PARADOX:
The Case for the Extraterrestrial Origin of Man

By the same author

THE INDESTRUCTIBLE IRISH
WHITE PAPERS OF AN OUTRAGED CONSERVATIVE
THE KEY

PARADOX:
The Case for the Extraterrestrial Origin of Man

JOHN PHILIP COHANE

CROWN PUBLISHERS, INC.,
NEW YORK

Printed in the United States of America
Published simultaneously in Canada by
General Publishing Company Limited

Designed by Ruth Kolbert Smerechniak

Library of Congress Cataloging in Publication Data

Cohane, John Philip.
    Paradox: The case for the extraterrestrial origin of man
    Bibliography: p.

Includes index.
    1. Man—Origin.   2. Interplanetary voyages.
*3. Darwin, Charles Robert, 1809-1882. 4. Civilization,
Ancient. I. Title.*
GN281.4.C64 1977   001.9'4   77-8506
ISBN 0-517-52938-6

The question of questions for mankind—the problem which underlies all others, and is more deeply interesting than any other—is the ascertainment of the place which Man occupies in nature and of his relations to the universe of things. Whence our race has come; what are the limits of our power over nature and of nature's power over us; to what goal we are tending; [these] are the problems which present themselves anew and with undiminished interest to every man born into the world.

—THOMAS HUXLEY, *Man's Place In Nature*

ACKNOWLEDGMENTS

A number of people who helped in this project are mentioned in the text and so are not included here. In addition, I wish to express my gratitude to Dr. Van L. Johnson, Professor of Classics (Retired), Tufts University, former General Secretary of the Archaeological Institute of America and former member of the American Philological Association, Honorary President of the American Classical League; Dr. Professor Johannes Rahder, Hall of Graduate Studies (Retired), Yale University; Dr. Frederick L. Santee, former Professor of Classics, Kenyon College; the late Dr. Fairfield Osborn, head of the New York Zoological Society and the American Conservation Foundation, who was the first to encourage me in this assignment; Herbert A. Kenny, longtime book editor of the *Boston Globe,* a pillar of strength at all times; Robert Musel, Senior Editor, UPI, London; Philip Weld, one of the world's great yachtsmen and a fund of practical information; William Hobby, Lieutenant Governor of Texas, and his wife, Diana; Barry Winkleman, in charge of atlas and gazetteer affairs at *The Times* (London); Robert F. Scott, former Director, the Library of Science, New York, and now Publisher, Stoeger Publishing Company; John Michell, a brilliant Eton and Cambridge graduate, whose books are so highly regarded by the young and open-minded old in England and America; Dr. Jeremiah Newman, Bishop of Limerick, earlier President of Maynooth College, Ireland; Dr. Walter F. Sheehan, former headmaster, the Canterbury School, New Milford, Connecticut; Colonel Sean O'Driscoll, USAF (Retired), Castle Matrix, Limerick; Dr. Hugh Kenner, distinguished author-critic, Professor of English, University of California at Santa Barbara, whose endorsement of my earlier book *The Key* helped propel me on this venture, as did Professor of English Victor Strite, Baylor University; Robert Kirsch, Book Critic, the *Los Angeles Times;* John O'Neill, Professor of English, Georgia Tech; Richard T. Crowe, Chicago author and antiquarian; Marilyn Vittert Lipman, the *St. Louis Post-Dispatch;* Charles McQueeny, Managing Editor, the *New Haven Evening Register;* William L. Essterling, Chairman of the Department of Foreign Languages, Armstrong State College, Savannah, Georgia; A. G. McKay, the *Houston Post;* John S. Gosnell, the *Virginia Pilot,* Norfolk; J. F. Rothermel, the *Birmingham News;* Phyllis Schwagerel, the *Sioux City Morning Journal;* Lewis Fisher, the *San Antonio Express-News;* C. L. Dancey, the *Peoria Morning Journal Star;* Malcolm Forsyth, the *New Orleans States-Item;* Paul Douglass, the *Orlando Sentinel;* Leonard Dubkin, *Skyline,* Chicago; John Webb, Creative Director of SSC & B (London); Patrick Campbell, the *Irish Echo,* New York; Douglas Gageby, former Editor, the *Irish Times;* Brendan Halligan, Editor, the *Limerick Leader;* Michael Hand, Editor, the *Sunday Independent* (Ireland), and Des Hickey, lead feature writer for the same newspaper.

I also wish to thank the superb staffs of the Science Reference Library, Bayswater, London, and the British Newspaper Library, Collingdale, London, where the bulk of the research was done in the pleasantest of surroundings; also the staffs of the British Museum Reading Room, the Royal Astronomical Library, London, the Trinity College Library and the National Library, both in Dublin; the New York Public Library, the Widener Library, Harvard University, the British Council Library, Rome, and the Limerick Public Library; also Messrs. McCann and Long of the Provincial Copying and Printing Company, Limerick, for technical assistance in the preparation of the maps. I also wish to thank Dr. Maxine Asher and her dedicated, intellectually curious fellow workers at the Ancient Mediterranean Research Association (AMRA), Los Angeles. To Paul Nadan, Senior Editor, Crown Publishers, my thanks for his objectivity, and to his Editorial Assistant, Susan Malsin, for her painstaking care with details.

The maps appearing on pages 122 to 136 were executed by Professor Michael Meehan, head of the Department of Geography, Thomond College, Limerick. The author is also grateful to the following:

The Sunday *Times* (London) for permission to reprint excerpts from articles by Julian Huxley and others which originally appeared in the

Sunday *Times'* "Destiny of Man" series during the summer of 1958.

And also to the Sunday *Times* for permission to reprint excerpts from an article by Michael Pye on the lost civilization of Meroe.

The Boston *Globe* and its staff reporter Robert Cooke for permission to use portions of Mr. Cooke's feature on early Egypto-Libyan voyages in the South Pacific and decipherments of inscriptions relating to these voyages made by Professor Barry Fell of Harvard.

Also the Boston *Globe* for permission to reproduce a map which accompanied this feature.

United Press International for permission to include excerpts from a UPI release dealing with the decipherment of a pre-Columbian stone from Bourne, Mass., also by Dr. Fell.

The *Sunday Express* (London; Robert Chapman, Science Editor) for permission to reprint excerpts from Mr. Chapman's article on Sirius-B which first appeared in that newspaper.

The Associated Press for permission to reprint in toto an AP release from Mountain View, California, describing space colonies proposed by Dr. Gerald K. O'Neill of Princeton University and associates.

Harper & Row, New York, for permission to reprint portions of *Secrets of the Great Pyramid* by Peter Tompkins. Copyright © 1971 by Peter Tompkins.

And to Dr. Roger W. Wescott, Professor of Anthropology and Linguistics, Drew University, Madison, New Jersey, also President, LACUS (Linguistic Association of Canada and the United States), for permission to use four paragraphs from his lecture "Interhemispheric Travel before the Vikings," delivered at a Drew Graduate School Aquinas Seminar in 1975.

There are today in many conceivably related areas of knowledge an extraordinary number of facts that cannot be fitted into the accepted version of our origin, ancestry, prehistory, and early history.

Certain of these wide-ranging facts are well known to the public; others are not. Apparently no one has assembled a significant number of them in one place in order to examine them as an entity, to see if they add up to conclusions that may differ radically from the current scientific consensus.

If this effort proves successful, the framework of a hypothesis should take shape within which many other known nonconforming facts will fit.

CHAPTER

1

A little over a century ago, for the first time in nearly two thousand years, the human race was offered a compelling alternate choice to the Genesis version of Creation, which held that an Almighty God had about six thousand years ago during seven days brought into existence the world and all living creatures in it including man. This alternate version was the theory of evolution.

What follows is in no way an attack on, nor even a general questioning of, that theory. There is no quarrel with the age of the universe and of this planet as scientifically accepted today, nor with the millions of years that it took for *Homo sapiens* to evolve as a species.

What does appear self-evident is that during the twentieth century, at an ever-increasing, often bewildering pace, new facts—not available to Charles Darwin, Thomas Huxley, and Ernst Haeckel and their disciples—have accumulated which have drastically changed our concept not only of the universe but especially of man's place in it.

These facts fall into three broad categories:

1. What is now known about prehistoric man and early

1

historic man—the swiftly unfolding record of what *Homo sapiens* has accomplished on this planet during the past ten thousand years (the so-called Holocene period).

2. What is now known about the universe that surrounds us.

3. What is now known, or perhaps more aptly, *not* known about the origin and ancestry of *Homo sapiens* prior to the Holocene period.

On these three vital, closely related fronts the picture has changed beyond recognition from what it was in the Huxley/Haeckel heyday of a century ago, when—working of necessity from a limited *terrestrial* perspective and with no real knowledge of early man—scientists rigidly established the essential evolutionary dictums that still hold sway.

On the first front, one hundred years ago a vicious battle, spearheaded by the Vatican, was being waged in Rome to prevent the excavation of the Forum for fear the faith of the masses might be weakened if they learned that mere "pagans" had wrought such wonders.

Behind the golden age so well loved by more broad-minded classicists stretched a bleak wasteland inhabited solely by wild animals and ignorant barbarians. Troy and Mycenae, to the astonishment of most and the consternation of many whose credo taught that "primitive" man was incapable of achieving anything of importance, were only just emerging out of the mists of legend.

Today, with archaeological and related discoveries taking place all over the earth—hardly a month passes without new key facts added to our knowledge of early man—it is impossible to remain any longer straitjacketed within the outdated Darwinian concept of prehistoric wandering creatures one step removed from caves and bogs and two steps from the apes. It is impossible to remain straitjacketed even in spite of vigorous efforts to maintain this Darwinian illusion deemed so essential to the central theory of man's terrestrial evolution.

On the second front, the universe around us, there is today not the slightest resemblance to what Thomas Huxley described as the "abyss of space." Aside from the fact that *Homo sapiens* has proved he can leave this planet's orbit, we now know that the sun is only one of 100 billion stars in our galaxy, the Milky Way, and that the Milky Way is only one of 100 billion galaxies in the universe.

When Harlow Shapley of the Harvard Observatory some years ago stunned the scientific world, let alone the public, by announcing that he and his associates believed there were probably 100 million inhabited planets in the universe—on two-thirds of which, based on the ages of other stars, there are probably intelligent beings more advanced than ourselves—he was talking about one one-thousandth of one percent of the estimated number of planets in the universe.

And when the equally distinguished astronomer Otto Struve expressed the belief that there may be one billion inhabited planets in the Milky Way alone, he was still talking about only one percent of the estimated total.

Only an extremely hard-backed traditionalist would deny that our present knowledge of the universe adds at least some potential new dimension to the question of *Homo sapiens'* origin and ancestry, certainly as compared to a century ago.

One can only speculate, for example, on the reactions if at that momentous Linnaean Society meeting in 1858 when Charles Darwin presented his preliminary paper on the origin of species he had spoken the following sentences:

> Any civilization capable of communicating with earth from another planet would unquestionably be older than man's. It would have long since mastered the problems that now plague the earth; pollution, overpopulation, and the ever-present threat of war would surely be a part of its past. And if it had learned to control the awesome power of the technology that it surely must possess, perhaps it would teach that secret of survival to man.

Although "survival" was Darwin's principal topic that evening, on such terms it would have been totally incomprehensible to both the speaker and his distinguished audience. Yet, when these sentences appeared in *Time* magazine's cover story, "Looking For Life Out There" (December 13, 1971), they were understood and accepted as logical by thousands of readers who had been conditioned to them by fourteen years of man's ventures beyond the environs of the earth, as well as by our rapidly expanding knowledge of the universe.

Is it mere coincidence that, couched in old-fashioned, pre-Darwinian language, *Time*'s observations in essence add up to the following statement: "Salvation may come to those living in this vale of tears through the intervention of wiser beings who dwell in heaven"? Is there an indication that when the Genesis version of Creation was (quite rightly) discarded in favor of the theory of evolution, man's ancient knowledge of the true state of affairs in the world around us was (quite wrongly) also dismissed as fantasy? Wheat tossed aside with the chaff?

Time was speculating on something that might happen in the future. Despite outraged screams from some quarters, Erich Von Däniken, when he posed the question "Was God an Astronaut?" was only speculating on what might have happened in the past. But both represent an updating of the traditional metaphysical position, based on recently discovered scientific data that were totally unfamiliar to Darwin, Huxley, and Haeckel.

Not long ago a fourteen-year-old student remarked: "I don't know much about outer space, but flying saucers make more sense to me than all that stuff about God and heaven and the angels." He could have been speaking the uninhibited, unconditioned language of the future.

Much has been written about our newly acquired knowledge of early man and of the universe. In themselves neither offers conclusive evidence that the evolution of *Homo sapiens* as a species over many millions of years might have taken place somewhere other than on this planet.

With the launching of *Sputnik I* nearly twenty years ago, however, the new data accumulating on those two related fronts, early man and the universe, made the current evidence regarding man's terrestrial evolution a matter of ever-increasing importance.

Given a situation in which it is as difficult today to question any major tenet of Darwinism as it was in the mid-nineteenth century for the Darwinians to challenge prevailing religious dogma, this above facet of the overall subject has not been explored in any depth, nor has it been homogenized within the three broad categories we've considered and examined as a whole. And yet it is the paramount issue as far as man's place in the universe is concerned.

A thorough study of this evidence reveals the little known fact that the orthodox version of *Homo sapiens'* terrestrial evolution as put forth by Darwin, Huxley, and Haeckel has been radically changed from what it was in their day. It has become unrecognizable in many respects by comparison with what was taught in American universities only forty years ago—to such a degree that if the current scientific consensus on man's terrestrial evolution had been propounded as a new theory during the last century, it would probably have caused scarcely a ripple in academic circles, and at best would have brought forth only a few polite yawns from the public.

The picture today is so full of unanswered, apparently insoluble riddles, so paradoxical in its nature, that to accept without question the theory that man evolved on this planet calls for almost as much faith as was asked of those who for so many centuries blindly accepted the Genesis version of Creation.

If nothing else, it is a picture that should be pulled out from the shadows and at last exposed to the public to help them decide whether, once again, as so often in the past, they have been led astray, wittingly or unwittingly, by the powers that be.

One hundred years before Darwin, the eighteenth-century French scientist Buffon, who unlike Lavoisier escaped the guillotine by dying in his bed the year before the Bastille fell, established what has become the orthodox Darwinian position of man in relation to the other primates. Buffon wrote:

> As regards the orang-utan's body, he differs less from man than he does from other animals which are still called apes.

Darwin's first major work, published in 1859, *On the Origin of Species by Means of Natural Selection, or the Preservation of Favoured Races in the Struggle for Life*—a title ominous with overtones of what the future would wreak upon mankind—did not include *Homo sapiens* as part of the overall evolutionary scheme of things.

Influenced in part by his wife's strong religious convictions and possibly by his own early training for the clergy, aware too that controversy would boil primarily around the question of *Homo sapiens'* relationship to the rest of the animal kingdom, Darwin limited his views to the statement: "Light will be thrown on the origin of man and his history."

In editions that followed the first—an instant success with 1250 copies sold out in 24 hours—this was changed to read: "*Much* light, etc." Darwin would probably have been content to let the matter rest but not so Thomas Huxley.

Four years later, in 1863, with the publication of *Evidence as to Man's Place in Nature,* against the advice of Sir Charles Lyell and other staunch supporters, Huxley tackled the major issue head on. One finds Buffon's dictum dressed in slightly different garb:

Whatever system of organs be studied, the comparison of their modifications in the ape series leads to one and the same result—that the structural differences which separate Man from the Gorilla and the Chimpanzee are not as great as those which separate the Gorilla from the lower apes (i.e. monkeys).

Elsewhere in the same book Huxley described apes as being merely "blurred copies" of man.

Ernst Haeckel, when he joined the front rank of those propagandizing the "New Religion," took Huxley's dictum by courtesy of Buffon and labeled it the "Huxleyan Law, or Pithecometra Thesis," and as such it was presented to the world.

The Establishment had already more or less swallowed Lyell's *Principles of Geology* (1830–33), which started the ball rolling toward a drastic backdating of the earth's age. They might even have sat still for an evolutionary process akin to the one proposed by Darwin's grandfather, the Rev. Erasmus Darwin,* but Huxley shoved the third and bitterest pill of all squarely down their protesting throats. The human race was descended from monkeys and apes.

It is little wonder that Mrs. Tait, the wife of the Archbishop of Canterbury, after roundly condemning this devil incarnate, concluded in disbelief: "And yet I hear that he is a devoted husband and affectionate father."

Although still hesitant and retiring, Darwin was sufficiently encouraged by the reception given to his disciple's book by the non-Establishment to complete *The Descent of Man, and Selection in Relation to Sex,* which was published in 1871. In it he threw the weight of his not inconsiderable worldwide reputation behind Huxley: "We may infer that some ancient member of the anthromorphous [i.e. anthropoid-ape] subgroup gave birth to man," he stated.

The die was cast, irrevocably. The "Huxleyan Law or Pithecometra Thesis" became the basis for explaining man's place in nature. Supported by the two works of Darwin, it went on to conquer the nations of the earth.

Huxley, joined in 1874 by Haeckel, devoted the rest of his life until

---

* In 1794 Erasmus Darwin had written: "The world has been evolved, not created; it has arisen little by little from a small beginning, and has increased through the activity of the elemental forces embodied in itself; and so has rather grown than come into being at an almighty word." Although the statement might well have come from the grandson, it scarcely lifted an eyebrow in the late eighteenth century.

his death in 1894, twelve years after Darwin's, to a vigorous public championing of his master's views, both in Europe and America, where he became the darling of the lecture halls, his influence without parallel.

When Huxley and Haeckel (in 1919) passed from the terrestrial scene, each must have thought his mission had been successfully accomplished, that what lay ahead would consist mainly in minor refinements of their teachings. At the Fourth International Congress of Zoology at Cambridge in 1898 Haeckel closed his address as follows:

> Looking forward to the twentieth century, I am convinced that it will universally accept our theory of descent, and that future science will regard it as the greatest advance made in our times.

It was a conviction Haeckel cherished until his death. Building on the cornerstone that *Homo sapiens* was "structurally" more closely related to the gorilla and chimpanzee than to other lower primates, he perfected the idea of an "ascending scale of the living primates culminating in Man." He also popularized the "family tree" concept of organic relationships, which is still firmly implanted in the minds of millions of people.

On the surface it would appear that today all is well in the orthodox Darwinian camp. Thousands of students all over the world start out their courses in organic evolution by reading Huxley's *Man's Place in Nature,* reinforcing the so-called infallibility of the Huxleyan Law.

One interesting article in this direction ran in the August/ September 1975 issue of *Natural History,* a popular magazine published by New York City's American Museum of Natural History.

Entitled "Man and Other Animals," it was written by Stephen Jay Gould, Professor of Geology at Harvard, and appeared in his regular column, "This View of Life." It read in part:

> The battle shifted long ago from a single debate about evolution: educated people now accept the evolutionary continuity between man and ape. . . .
> Many criteria have been tried, and one by one they have failed. The only honest alternative is to admit the strict continuity in kind between ourselves and chimpanzees. . . .
> We are more nearly akin to the chimpanzee than even Huxley dared to think. . . .

Huxley permanently dimmed the ardor of those seeking an anatomical discontinuity between man and ape. . . .
Few scientists have strongly pushed the anatomical argument since Owen's debacle. . . . [Gould is referring to the victory Thomas Huxley won over Richard Owen in the great hippocampus debate. Owen failed to establish man's uniqueness by arguing that the *hippocampus minor,* a small convolution of the brain, was found only in *Homo sapiens.*]

The above sentences would undoubtedly warm the hearts of Huxley and Haeckel if they could read them today, supporting the latter's conviction that the twentieth century would "universally accept" their "theory of descent." They are, however, *factually* totally incorrect. They are the direct antithesis of the truth.

Since the appearance of *Man's Place in Nature* and the Owen debate, no fewer than eleven of the world's most eminent comparative anatomists, anthropologists, and paleontologists—a number of them engaged in two or three of these disciplines—have taken vehement exception to the Huxleyan Law. Their combined viewpoints have slowly but drastically altered the positioning of man as established by Huxley and Haeckel without the news seeping through to the general public and, judging from Stephen Jay Gould's remarks, to some in the academic community.

Before presenting the written and recorded spoken views of these eleven scientists, which deal solely with the *structural* differences between man and other primates, it is worth turning *Homo sapiens* around for a moment and regarding him from the psychozoatic or physical–metaphysical angle. Thomas Huxley's grandson, Sir Julian Huxley, issued his own Buffon-style dictum a few years before his death in the early 1970s:

While the gorilla, chimpanzee, and orang-outang are the closest living relations of man, Humphrey Johnson graphically summed up the chasm between ourselves and our earthbound cousins when he wrote in 1943 that there was a greater difference between a man and a gorilla than between a gorilla and a daisy. One is as incapable as the other of creating a civilization.

We will return to the psychozoatic view later.
The structural opinions below are presented in chronological order

except for the first statements, which provide an excellent summation of the basic anti-Huxley/Haeckel position.

These statements emanated from Frederic Wood Jones, who in 1918, as Professor of Comparative Anatomy at Manchester University, became the leader of the opposition, a role he played for thirty years, next as Professor of Comparative Anatomy at London University, and finally, at the very pinnacle of his profession, as Professor of Human and Comparative Anatomy at the Royal College of Surgeons in London, a post he held from 1945 until two years before his death in 1954.

Frederic Wood Jones was the author of the two definitive works *The Hand* (1920) and *The Foot* (1944). W. C. Osman Hill, author of the monumental eight-volume standard reference work *The Primates,* refers to him in his preface as the most important single influence in his career. Scientists recently interviewed in London still regard him as without peer.

And yet his "unorthodox" opinions had to be pieced together over many months out of the files of the British Museum Reading Room and the superb Science Reference Library in Bayswater, London. The books, pamphlets, and lectures from which the following material was taken are rarely if ever listed in his bibliography.

1918–1948: Frederic Wood Jones: Having characterized the work of Haeckel as "perhaps without parallel for its blind dogmatism, its crudity of assertion, and its offensive discourtesy," he described Thomas Huxley as "far more subtle a thinker but nevertheless he produced the same popular results—he led people to think that man's origin along the final stages of the scale of life had been scientifically proved to be true."

Wood Jones blamed this primarily on the Huxleyan Law:

> It was the adoption of this law that shaped the whole of Huxley's work on the origin of man and more than this, it is by the handing on of this tradition that he has shaped the work of so many others.

Huxley wrongly reached the conclusion that "the terminal portion of the scale of life represented a true end-on evolution, that man, the anthropoid apes, the monkeys, the lemurs and the horizontal, four-footed mammals represented a true evolutionary series."

In two landmark addresses delivered in the spring of 1947, the first a

Linacre Lecture on May 6 at Cambridge University, the second an Anis and Gale Lecture on May 14 at the Royal College of Surgeons in London, Wood Jones concluded:

> If the primate forms immediately ancestral to the human stock are ever to be revealed [in 1977 as in 1947 no such ancestors of man have yet been found], they will be utterly unlike the slouching, hairy ape men of which some have dreamed and of which they have made casts and pictures during their waking hours, and they will be found in geological strata antedating the heyday of the great apes. . . .
> That man shows certain structural specializations that are absolute human distinctions is not to be doubted; and even the brief survey we have made of them is sufficient to show the fallacy of Huxley's anaesthetic dictum that the structural differences between man and the gorilla or chimpanzee are less than those that distinguish the anthropoids from the lower primates.

The adjective *anaesthetic* ("producing insensibility") is particularly well chosen.

Despite Stephen Jay Gould's statements that "Huxley permanently dimmed the ardor of those seeking an anatomical discontinuity between man and ape," and "Few scientists have strongly pushed the anatomical argument since Owen's debacle," the undiminished ardor and unflagging strength with which England's premier comparative anatomist pushed his basic arguments over three decades constitutes one of the most inspiring yet relatively unknown chapters in the history of science.

That Wood Jones's opinions prevail today as the "inner circle" scientific consensus will be demonstrated after presenting a few other highly pertinent observations he made in 1947 as well as reviewing what the ten other eminent scientists referred to have had to say about Huxley's views on man's place in nature.

CHAPTER

3

In one brilliant, succinct sentence Wood Jones struck at the very heart of the Huxley/Haeckel theory of man's descent:

> It is difficult to imagine how a being, whose body is replete with features of a basal mammalian simplicity, can have sprung from any of those animals in which so much of this simplicity has been lost.

The "brief survey" (it was not brief) conducted in Wood Jones's two 1947 lectures pointed out that structurally it was impossible for *Homo sapiens* to pass through a long-armed, knuckle-walking, brachiating (tree-swinging) stage, or originally to possess beetling brows and protruding jaws and then revert back to his present-day simplicity. A solid knowledge of comparative anatomy ruled out the possibility that the evolutionary process worked in opposite directions.

Equally important, it was anatomically impossible for the human foot to have evolved out of an apelike prehensile or grasping part of the body, which is more like a hand than a foot. Man's foot could only have reached its present specialized form after millions of years in an erect position—the all-important development that in turn led to the evolution of the unique human brain.

This was the direct antithesis of the Huxley/Haeckel theory that the upright position came near the end of *Homo sapiens'* evolution. The orthodox version mistakenly put the cart before the horse.*

---

* Wood Jones stated: "It was this adoption of an upright posture, coming as it must have done as an accomplished fact during a favorable phase of evolutionary development, that produced the profound changes, both quantitative and qualitative, that sever Man altogether from the assemblage of the Anthropoid Apes. . . .

The only explanation for man's unique hallmarks, Wood Jones concluded, was that he must have broken off from the primate stem many millions of years ago, pursuing his own evolutionary course apart from monkeys and apes—with no evolutionary continuity between man and ape, no strict continuity in kind between ourselves and chimpanzees. (See Professor Gould's remarks on discontinuity.)

Taking up in chronological order the views of the other leading scientists:

1869: Between the publication of *Man's Place in Nature* and Darwin's *The Descent of Man,* Dr. George W. Callender, also in his day Professor of Comparative Anatomy at the Royal College of Surgeons, wrote in a monograph (as quoted in Jones's *The Problem of Man's Ancestry*):

> Whereas in all anthropoid apes and monkeys, in common with the rest of animals, the anterior [front] part of the face is formed by the premaxillary bone, in Man alone is this bone overgrown by the Maxilla [upper jaw bone] and excluded from appearing on the face.

This was a far more serious challenge than the one put forward by Richard Owen but was not taken up by Huxley or Haeckel. Eventually it played a key role in the removal of two hot favorites from the list of man's ancestry— Neanderthal man and Australopithecus.

1873: Dr. St. George Mivart, Professory of Comparative Anatomy at St. Mary's College, London, Vice President of the Zoological Society, Fellow of the Royal Society. Mivart, whose definition of a primate still stands, wrote:

"Doubtless after the attainment of the functional change structural adaptations were perfected in order to remould certain parts to the demands in the alteration in posture. But to misinterpret these structural adaptations as indications of a gradual assumption of the posture is to abandon the great biological principle that function is the creator of structure."

Only through such an ancient achievement could there have been a changed relationship between the axis of the vertebral column and the basicranial axis allowing the globular enlargement of the braincase to take place. It was the "most important event that has ever occurred in the evolution of living things . . . [it] entailed an all-important change in the visual axis in relation to the free movements of the head and many other subsidiary adjustments without which it is difficult, if not impossible, to suppose that the typical cerebral distinctions of Man could have developed. . . .

"The human upright bipedal habit of posture and progression was certainly no by-product of any activity such as existing Anthropoid Apes display . . . it was not the product of the other human characteristics: it was the initiator of them all."

However near to apes may be the body of man, whatever the kind or number of resemblances between them, it should always be borne in mind that it is to no one kind of ape that man has any special affinities—that the resemblances between him and lower forms are shared in not very unequal proportions by different species. . . . There can be no question that at least such preponderance of resemblance is not presented by the much vaunted Gorilla, which is essentially no less a brute and no more a man than is the humblest member of the [primate] family to which it belongs.

Running directly counter to the Huxley/Haeckel concept, Mivart stated:

It is manifest that man, the apes, and half-apes cannot be arranged in a single ascending series of which man is the term and culmination. . . . The human structural characters are shared by so many and such diverse forms, that it is impossible to arrange even groups of genera in a single ascending series. . . . On any conceivable hypothesis there are many similar structures, each of which must be deemed to have been independently evolved in more than one instance.

It was the first all-important step toward sending man off millions of years ago on his own lonely evolutionary road. It also anticipated by nearly a century the concept of "parallel evolution" which is today a key tenet of scientific thought. Man does not possess any special affinities that are closer to the great apes than they are to monkeys, lemurs, or other early primate species.

Again, from the foremost comparative anatomist of his day, this was a direct contradiction of continuity between man and ape.

Only once in his book, *Man and Apes,* did Mivart momentarily lose his composure:

One of the most grotesque conceptions suggested by Mr. Darwin is that the nakedness of man, and especially of woman, has been produced by the gradual extension over the body (through the persistent choice of more and more hairless spouses) of an incipient local nakedness like that now existing in certain apes. No facts known to the author afford the slightest basis for this bizarre hypothesis.

No one has yet come up with a satisfactory explanation for human nakedness. Elsewhere in *The Origin of Species* Darwin declared: "Beards are products of sexual selection, intended as an ornament to charm and excite the opposite sex."

1896: E. D. Cope, the American paleontologist whose vast private collection formed the nucleus of the American Museum of Natural History, claimed in *The Origin of the Fittest* that man must have been "derived from a group represented by the fossil tarsoid," a creature that became extinct 40 to 60 million years ago.

The anthropoid apes, in Cope's opinion, had "sprung from the same source," but had followed their own separate evolutionary path—another complete *dis*continuity between man and ape.

Cope's line of reasoning, based on a profound firsthand knowledge of fossils, would make the present-day spectral tarsus—a small, arboreal, nocturnal creature with a long, thin tail and huge eyes, who resides in Indonesia and the Philippines—man's closest living relative, a thought that may prove unsettling to those who have grown accustomed to thinking they are descended from monkeys and apes.

A number of current books on evolution completely misrepresent Cope as an unswerving, orthodox disciple of Darwin, Huxley, and Haeckel. (See, for example, Wendt's *Before the Deluge.)*

1897: In *The Descent of the Primates,* the American embryologist A. A. W. Hübrecht expanded on Cope's views. He concluded:

> I would not feel justified in contradicting a hypothetic view . . . according to which a direct ancestor of the anthropoids and man . . . must have sprung directly from a Mesozoic insectivorous ancestor [70 million to 220 million years ago], small in size, but already more or less erect in posture, provided with a spacious brain cavity. . . . As to the erect posture, we are in no way obliged to follow the general belief that this has been a comparatively late acquirement of our ancestors [as previously mentioned, a key Huxley/Haeckel tenet] nor that they must needs have passed through a stage similar to the actual stage of one of our living anthropoid apes.

What is perhaps most fascinating about Dr. Hübrecht's views is that he alone among the scientists quoted suggested that *Homo sapiens,* a mammal, may have started his own separate evolutionary development *prior* to the agreed-upon Age of the Mammals (80 million years ago), springing from a "Mesozoic insectivorous ancestor" conceivably 140 million years before mammals first appeared on earth.

Though this offers immense problems in accepted evolutionary terms, it highlights the growing concern as to how a species with such an extraordinary nervous system as man's—far more complex than was suspected half a century ago—could possibly have evolved into his present form in the span of 80 million years, when certain insects with no more complicated systems took from 300 to 400 million years to reach their present development. While out of the mainstream of the views presented here, from another direction it raises the central question: "Could *Homo sapiens* have evolved over a far longer period than 80 million years in some other part of the universe?"

One other book of the nineteenth century deserves mention because, though it did not build directly toward the present scientific consensus, at the height of Ernst Haeckel's fame it indicated cautious doubt as to his infallibility by one of his own countrymen.

The book was *The Structure of Man, An Index to His Past History* (1895), written by Dr. R. Weidersheim, Professor of Anatomy at the University of Freiburg. His views were summed up as follows:

> I willingly admit that nothing is gained by the mere demonstration of "animal likenesses," and that the final and only satisfactory solution of the great riddle of Man must lie in the demonstration of his genealogy and the line of his inheritance. . . .
> Now that the African continent is being opened up, the scientific mind waits with longing for the careful investigation of its Tertiary Lacustrine deposits [lake deposits dating from one million to 70 million years ago]. Hugh Falconer predicted long ago that human remains would be forthcoming in the Tertiary deposits of India, and no one conversant with recent work in Mammalian Paleontology would doubt that the remains of ancestral Man must be sought this far back in time.

It was a fervent longing which, in spite of dedicated searching for nearly a century, has never been fulfilled. We will shortly find Professor Lord Zuckerman, chief scientific adviser to both Conservative and Labour governments in the 1960s, expressing doubt in 1954 that there will ever be a discovery of an "indisputable series of 'missing links' in a fossil lineage," and in 1961 Professor Philip G. Fothergill, Department of Botany, King's College, Newcastle-upon-Tyne (who was the second person to encourage me in this essentially reportorial task), stated somewhat wistfully in *Evolution and Christians:*

The discovery of Tertiary man would be an event of outstanding importance.

For the first time we come face to face with the most baffling paradox of all time: The consensual scientific opinion today is that man must have broken off from the primate stem at least 30 million years ago, conceivably much earlier, and yet the same consensual scientific opinion does not accept that there is a single fossil trace of man from 500,000 to 70 million years ago.

Nor is the situation any more satisfactory for the past half million years. As of today, no accepted, proven ancestor of *Homo sapiens* has been discovered anywhere on the face of this planet.

It is not just a question of a "missing link"; the whole chain is missing.

Continuing into the twentieth century:

1911–1922: During the period from before World War I until the early 1920s the field work of Pierre Marcellin Boule, Director of the French Museum of Natural History, provided a sizable bulk of evidence that eventually played a vital role in the anti-Huxley/Haeckel interpretation of man's origin and ancestry.

Much of this evidence, which was concerned primarily with remains of Neanderthal man unearthed at La Chapelle-aux-Saints, was published between 1911 and 1913.* A decade later up-to-date findings appeared in *Les Hommes Fossiles* (Masson & Cie, Paris, 1921).

The priceless data contained in Boule's principal work remained untranslated into English for the next forty-six years until Thames and Hudson brought out an edition in London, *Fossil Men,* by Boule and H. V. Vallois.

The French paleontologist concluded from his extensive research that man had "been derived neither from the Anthropoid [ape] stem, nor from any other known group, but from a very ancient Primate stock that separated from the main line even before the giving off of the Lemuroids."

This family, which evolved on its own 60 million to 70 million years ago, is represented today by a variety of lemurs that dwell almost exclusively in Madagascar. The "Lost Continent of Mu," of which

---

* See "L'homme fossile de la Chapelle-aux-Saints," *Annales de Paléontologie* 6: 109–72; 7: 85–192; 8: 1–67.

Madagascar is claimed to be a vestige, derives its name from le*mur*.

Boule maintained that the only logical conclusion to his findings, couched in simple language, was that the human branch of evolution was independent of neighboring branches, notably of that leading to the anthropoid ape.

Here one finds the foremost French evolutionist of this century disclaiming entirely any continuity between man and ape—chimpanzee, gorilla, or whatever.

It is understandable why my generation was taught at Yale and other universities in the early 1930s that *Homo sapiens* evolved directly from Neanderthal man. But in the light of what has happened since then, it is surprising to find the late J. Bronowski in his magnificent study *The Ascent of Man* holding him up forty years later as one of the two proven, accepted ancestors of the human race.

The majority of specialists today would not concur in this opinion. See as one example among many Philip Fothergill's *Evolution and Christians:* "It is a fact commonly admitted that the neanderthaloids did not give rise to *Homo sapiens,* but that they form a side branch from an earlier stem." Similar views are presented further on.

Mr. Bronowski's other choice, Australopithecus (c. one million years ago), is equally difficult to understand. Some years before *The Ascent of Man* was published, in the Sunday London newspaper *The Observer* (January 23, 1966), Dr. Louis B. Leakey, the indefatigable discoverer (with his wife, Mary) of most of the Australopithecine fossils, was quoted:

> They were not ancestors of man, but an evolutionary sideline.*

Today millions of readers of Bronowski, Robert Ardrey *(African Genesis,* etc.), Ernest Wendt, and many other, less influential writers still clutch to their breasts as their ancestor the child that has been disowned by its own father.

The suspicion grows that while facts running counter to the public view of Darwinism often are suppressed, ignored, or distorted, any that support it are welcome, no matter how incorrect they may be, if

---

* The same article comments: "A mere 70,000 years ago, come the remains of Neanderthal man, who was once considered the immediate ancestor of *Homo sapiens,* but is nowadays agreed to be a specialized sideline which led to extinction."

they provide "foundation stones" that shore up the "stability of a building so familiar and so generally admired."

By the mid-1920s the first half century of propagandizing by the orthodox Darwinians had been amazingly successful. However, a period of reassessment had begun which slowly but increasingly allowed the expression of views that contradicted or questioned, at least in specific details, the Huxley/Haeckel hard line. The battle cry, "If you're against Darwin, you're against evolution," became temporarily muted.

And then in 1925 an event that was ridiculous in nature but which had wide-ranging, long-lasting consequences took place in the United States. It set the whole popular and, to a large extent, the academic community's, concept of evolution back fifty years. The event still casts its shadows over any objective assessment of man's true place in the universe.

On May 9, 1925, John T. Scopes, the science teacher and athletic coach of Rhea County High School in Dayton, Tennessee, was arrested for violating the State Anti-Evolution Law.

Now personally, I like Bill [William Jennings Bryan],
but when he says that he will make this his life's issue and take it up
through all the various courts
and finally endeavor to get it into the Constitution of the United States
and make a political and presidential issue out of it,
he is wrong.
More wrong than he has ever been before.
These other things he was wrong on didn't do much harm,
but now he is going to try to drag something
that pertains to the Bible into a political campaign.
He can't ever do that.
He might make Tennessee the side show of America,
but he can't make a street carnival out of the whole United States.

—WILL ROGERS on the Scopes "Monkey Trial"

The Judge ought to give 'em [the experts] a chance
to tell what evolution is.
'Course we got 'em licked anyhow,
but I believe in being fair and square and American.
Besides, I'd like to know what evolution is myself.

—REP. JOHN WASHINGTON BUTLER,
author of the Tennessee Anti-Evolution Bill

Evolution, as far as the masses were concerned, came fully into its own
during July, 1925, at the red-bricked county courthouse in Dayton,
Tennessee. A sweltering heat wave was in progress, which had even
the two thousand inhabitants of that normally peaceful Cumberland
mountain town mopping their sun-scorched brows and fanning
themselves.

Surrounded by the same hoopla that was to attend the Dempsey-Tunney world heavyweight championship fight in Philadelphia the following year and the Lindbergh ticker-tape welcome-home to New York in 1927, the news media from both sides of the Atlantic—editors, columnists, cartoonists, reporters, photographers, radio broadcasters—swarmed to the scene. Within two weeks the name "Darwin" had become a household word throughout the English-speaking countries and well beyond.

Those who couldn't read or afford radios learned the big news from their neighbors that they were descended from monkeys. "Darwin was right!" became overnight a shout of derision hurled back and forth among children from coast to coast.

J. R. Darwin, who owned a ready-to-wear emporium on the main street of Dayton, was the happiest man in town. He strung a big banner across the front of his store: "DARWIN IS RIGHT—INSIDE!"

Monkeys provided the dominant theme of the swirling sideshow. Along with hot dogs, lemonade, Bibles, popcorn, peanuts, and chewing gum, toy simian souvenirs were brisk items at stands set up along the steaming sidewalks. Colorful posters of monkeys and coconuts adorned the windows of many shops. "Your Old Man's a Monkey!" became another popular youthful national challenge.

What student of that era will ever forget as long as he lives the thrill of witnessing almost from a ringside seat the methodical way in which Clarence Darrow diminished the bumbling Fundamentalist William Jennings Bryan, who succumbed the Sunday after the trial from emotional exhaustion, the heat wave, and too big a noontime dinner? Could a person with common sense any longer deny where the truth lay? Even those who weren't at all sure there was a God wondered if the hand of God weren't in it somewhere.

A few lines from the courtroom testimony should suffice to show what sort of defender of the faith Bryan made, this hitherto magnificent platform orator who had three times been a candidate for the U.S. Presidency and who served as Secretary of State in Woodrow Wilson's first cabinet:

Darrow: "You have never had any interest in the age of the various races and peoples and civilizations and animals that exist upon the earth today?"

Bryan: "I have never had any interest in the effort that has been made to dispute the Bible by the speculations of men or the investigations of men."

Darrow: "And you never have investigated to find out how long man has been on the earth?"

Bryan: "I have never found it necessary."

Darrow: "Don't you know that the ancient civilizations of China are six thousand or seven thousand years old, at the very least?"

Bryan: "No, but they would not run back beyond the Creation. According to the Bible, six thousand years."

Darrow: "What about the religion of Confucius or Buddha? Do you regard them as competitive?"

Bryan: "No, I think they are very inferior."

Darrow: "Mr. Bryan, am I the first man you ever heard of who has been interested in the age of human societies and primitive man?"

Bryan: "You are the first man I ever heard speak of the number of people at those different periods."

Darrow: "You have never in all your life made any attempt to find out about the other peoples of the earth—how old their civilizations are, how long they have existed on the earth—have you?"

Bryan: "No sir, I have been so well satisfied with the Christian religion that I have spent no time trying to find arguments against it. I have all the information I want to live by and to die by."

Actually, Darrow's cross-questioning of Bryan never got to the subject of evolution. The aging statesman came off so badly on the literal interpretation of such miracles as Jonah and the whale, and Joshua making the sun stand still, not to mention the earth's age and the known history of man, that the next day Judge John Raulston refused to let him back on the stand, ordered his evidence to be struck from the records, and instructed the jury to bring in a verdict.

John Scopes was found guilty and fined $100 for breaking a law that was on the state statute books, but public opinion was so clearly on the side of the defense that never again was the right to teach the theory of evolution tested in a court.

(In 1929, with the Scopes Trial still fresh in people's minds, it was argued before a St. Louis, Missouri, judge that the theory of evolution conferred on an ape a legal status that prohibited his being regarded as property. The judge disallowed the plea.)

Anti-evolution laws were pending in fifteen other states, and with the Fundamentalists organized behind Bryan to undertake a nation-wide step-by-step drive similar to the forcing through of the Eighteenth "Prohibition" Amendment, the Scopes Trial served an extremely useful purpose by stopping this campaign in its tracks.

The publicity given to the trial also aroused in many ordinary people for the first time a keen desire to know about their past, about evolution and the origin of man. Unfortunately it also had certain disastrous consequences.

The very fact that the Fundamentalists were shouting so loudly, "Man is *not* descended from monkeys and apes," caused their opponents to shout back just as loudly, "Man *is* descended from monkeys and apes."

Reassessments were buried under a fresh wave of what can best be described as "fundamentalist" evolutionary doctrine. The marketplace was flooded with books, pamphlets, and articles written by scientists and pseudoscientists anxious to cash in on the unprecedented public interest. In an emotional, Jesuitical "end-justifying-the-means" spirit, serious scholars condoned any material, no matter how faulty in detail, that supported the overall theory of evolution.

Looking back on the period some twenty years later—a period which had by no means ended in the 1940s, and obviously has not yet ended—Wood Jones wrote:

This [the Scopes Trial] may appear to be a trivial incident in the story of our ideas concerning the origin of Man, but it had a very definite effect in that it produced a spate of American literature written in the same spirit and directed towards the same ends as the numerous semi-popular publications produced by Huxley, Haeckel and the other Darwinian propagandists more than half a century before.

Many American zoologists and anthropologists conceived that the battle for evolution and especially for the Anthropoid Ape ancestry of Man had to be fought all over again. All the old dogmatism reappeared in its original form; but it derived an added source of strength from the easy acceptance of every additional piece of evidence presumed to be provided by all the paleontological relics unearthed in the interval.

Even after the passing of more than twenty years since the Dayton episode, many leading American authorities have not emancipated themselves from their emotional reaction to the not inconsiderable influence of the fundamentalists.

Many of the lessons and most of the cautions learned during the period of critical consideration that marked the first quarter of the twentieth century seem to have been forgotten. There has been a return to the age of dogmatism.

Singled out for special attention was a summation passage written in 1934 by the U.S. evolutionist Dr. W. K. Gregory in *Man's Place among the Anthropoids:*

> Meanwhile the enormous progress in modern genetics, endocrinology, embryology and allied sciences is beginning to give us some hints into the nature of physico-chemical forces that have moulded a mere tailless monkey into a being that makes gods of his own image and sweeps the heavens and the earth with a more than ape-like curiosity.

This was described as "doubtless a very stimulating passage and one well calculated to bring about the downfall of the last stronghold of fundamentalism, but it is one that is somewhat vulnerable in that it leads the reader to believe that it is a well-established fact that a 'mere tailless monkey' was at some time moulded into a man and that today the growing perfection of science is revealing the actual 'physico-chemical forces that brought about this moulding.'"

Nor was an embarrassing episode in 1922 overlooked, in which Gregory and his associate, Dr. M. Hellman, triumphantly proclaimed that a tooth of the so-called *Hesperopithecus haroldcooki* came from an "American Pliocene Anthropoid Ape" that, conforming to the Huxleyan Law, resembled "the human type more closely than it does any anthropoid ape." The tooth turned out to be from a peccary, a two-foot-high, four-footed, hooved, piglike creature that inhabits the Americas but is not even a member of the primate family.

1927: As the turmoil in the wake of the Scopes Trial mounted, without any advance warning the U.S. evolutionist who towered head and shoulders above all others, who was universally and affectionately acclaimed throughout the scientific world as "the Darwin and Huxley of America," suddenly folded up his tent and strode over to the opposition camp, the unorthodox outpost established by Callender, Mivart, Cope, Hübrecht, Boule, and Wood Jones.

Described by the latter as the only well-known American scientist who "remained conspicuously aloof from the growing challenge of the fundamentalists," who did not "permit an emotional reaction to their propaganda to affect his attitude of philosophic doubt regarding the positive claims of some of the more articulate of his colleagues," Dr. Henry Fairfield Osborn, the most famous of all directors of the American Museum of Natural History in New York, wrote in 1927 the first in a series of articles that sharply attacked the Huxley/ Haeckel version of man's origin and ancestry.

In Osborn's opinion their orthodox theory of descent had been "greatly weakened by recent evidence." Without equivocation he expressed the conviction that there must have been an "independent line of Dawn Man ancestors springing from an Oligocene [25 to 40 million years old] neutral stock, which also gave rise independently to the anthropoid apes."

In a complete reversal of his former position, his ardor in no way dimmed by Huxley from "seeking an anatomical discontinuity between man and ape," Osborn stated that on the basis of the new evidence he believed the line of man's descent had followed its own separate path for many millions of years. He further predicted that Oligocene fossil "pro-men with pro-human rather than pro-anthropoid limbs" would be discovered, a prediction that (complicating further the riddle of man's origin and pointing at least toward an even earlier separate ancestry) has not after half a century come true, and may never.

Osborn's first article, "Recent Discoveries Relating to the Origin and Antiquity of Man," appeared in *Science* (65: 481–88) magazine. A series of papers followed in rapid succession, each hammering home the same basic viewpoint. Until his death eight years later in 1935, the "Darwin and Huxley of America" vigorously chopped away at the underpinnings of the edifice which during most of his life he had done so much to strengthen.

Chancing upon Osborn's recantation in the Science Reference Library (a branch of the British Museum, London) created a particularly strong shock in this writer, for during the early 1930s at Yale my generation was taught solid Huxley/Haeckel organic evolution by Dr. R. N. Lull, himself a dedicated Osbornist. A number of Osborn's principles, notably his Law of Adaptive Radiation, were prominently featured, but never at any time was there the slightest whisper about his post-1926 opinions. He is still portrayed today in numerous popular books as a hardy traditionalist. Whether or not Stephen Jay Gould and the editor of *Natural History* are aware of what he wrote during his last eight years is a question only they can answer.

Closely tied in was a second, in some ways even more profoundly disturbing, shock. Drilled into us neophytes as one of the principal tenets of the new catechism—in fact the single most memorable proof of man's origin and ancestry—was another Haeckel-devised dictum:

"Ontogeny repeats phylogeny," i.e., the individual during the embryonic period, the time spent in the womb from conception to birth, repeats the entire evolutionary history of the phylum to which it belongs.

From discussions with a number of extremely well-educated men and women, including several medical practitioners, of a later vintage than mine, it would appear that "Ontogeny repeats phylogeny" maintained its exalted position at least into the mid-1950s.

And yet, in 1940 Sir G. B. de Beer in *Embryos and Ancestors* tore this dictum to shreds, to such a conclusive extent that in 1956 one finds C. H. Waddington in *Principles of Embryology* setting down the subverted scientific consensus as follows:

> The type of analogical thinking which leads to theories that development [in the embryo] is based on the recapitulation of ancestral stages or the like no longer seems at all convincing or even very interesting to biologists.

Unfortunately, telegrams have not been sent out to the many thousands of people who still walk around secure in the belief that ontogeny repeats phylogeny. Not long ago I mentioned casually to a lifelong friend and fellow university classmate that this particular dictum had adroitly been removed as an evolutionary foundation stone and quietly tossed into the ashcan.

It almost ended our friendship; his reaction was comparable to that of a devout Roman Catholic advised that the Virgin Birth has been refuted. Red-faced, he escorted me to the front door of the club where we were lunching, hoarsely whispering again and again, "Ontogeny *does* repeat phylogeny."

Such is the power of deeply implanted propaganda, no matter whether faith in science or religion is involved.

1946: Nineteen years after Osborn's about-face, his close friend and fellow worker, Robert Broom, who played a key role in the early Australopithecine findings (many of which ended up in the American Museum of Natural History), went on record as follows:

> The view supported in the present work is that the line which led to Man and the Australopithecines arose in Lower Oligocene or possibly Upper Eocene times from a pre-Anthropoid. This view is essentially similar to that of Osborn

and probably near to that of Wood Jones. [Wood Jones commented dryly the next year: "A cleavage that took place during the Eocene period some 50 or 60 million years ago cannot be described as recent even in geological terms."]

These words, written by Robert Broom five years before his death, have been as completely ignored as the latter-day opinions of Henry Fairfield Osborn. Especially in view of Dr. Louis B. Leakey's 1966 statement that the Australopithecines "were not ancestors of man, but an evolutionary sideline," it is a bit difficult to swallow, let alone digest the following passage from Ernest Wendt's *Before the Deluge* (p. 355):

> Up to his death in 1951 Broom remained a specialist on connections between the different stocks of animals. One of his books bears the arresting title *Finding the Missing Link*. By "missing link" Broom did not mean a mammal-like reptile, but a group of half-ape, half-human creatures (Australopithecines) whose remains he had blasted out of the limestone caves of South Africa. These *prehominids* were perhaps the most important fossil finds of recent decades. They were important for anthropologists, philosophers, and theologians as well as zoologists, for they established the long-sought bridge between animal and man whose existence Darwin had predicted.

Under the circumstances is it unfair to classify the above as science fiction? One is not surprised to find a subsequent, also extremely popular book by Wendt entitled *From Ape to Adam: The Search for the Evolution of Man,* with an especially lurid but familiar dust jacket portraying a long-armed ape walking on his knuckles, then half raised, next three-quarters erect with shortened arms and manly overtones, and finally, gloriously erect on his own two feet—man, or in this case apparently Adam. Structurally, an evolutionary impossibility.*

---

* The anatomical differences between man and ape that could only have resulted from an extremely ancient *dis*continuity between the two are graphically pointed up by the ape's habit of knuckle-walking. As any observant mother knows, a human infant invariably puts the palms of his hands flat on the ground or floor with the fingers extended, never flexing the digits and placing the knuckles down. It is structurally impossible for an ape to emulate a human on this score. Unlike ourselves, he cannot simultaneously flex the joints of his fingers, his wrist, and his elbow.

In 1949 one of the most significant of all documents on *Homo sapiens'* evolution appeared in the *Quarterly Review of Biology*. Entitled "The Riddle of Man's Ancestry," it was written by Dr. William L. Straus, Jr., Professor of Comparative Anatomy at the Johns Hopkins School of Medicine.

Although at the time it exerted a profound influence on both sides of the Atlantic, it too appears to have been forgotten in the seemingly never-ending flood of Huxley/Haeckel-oriented literature. Having briefly reviewed the work of his unorthodox predecessors, Dr. Straus put his own stamp of approval on *dis*continuity between man and ape:

> It is concluded that available evidence indicates that the line leading to man became independent at a relatively early date, probably no later than the end of the Oligocene period [25 to 40 million years ago], and that the stock from which it arose was essentially monkey-like rather than anthropoid-like.

In two unequivocal passages Dr. Straus summed up the existing situation regarding the evolution of *Homo sapiens,* and it is a summation even more pertinent to today than to 1949:

> Recent years have witnessed the discovery of a considerable number of fossil hominids, many of them obviously more primitive than modern man, and of numerous fossils of other primates. But these, instead of simplifying the phylogenetic story, have merely served to demonstrate its complexity, so that the apparent course of man's evolution is actually more obscure than it was for a few decades past. It is noteworthy, moreover, that forms intermediate between the human and

any of the other primate groups, forms popularly termed "missing links," are as conspicuous by their absence as they were in Darwin's day. . . .

What I wish especially to stress is that the problem of man's ancestry is still a decidedly open one, in truth, a riddle. Hence it ill behooves us to accept any premature verdict as final and so to prejudice analysis and interpretation of whatever paleontological material may come to light, as the orthodox theory has so often done and is still doing. One cannot assume that man is a made over anthropoid ape of any sort, for much of the available evidence is strongly against that assumption.

1954: Five years after the appearance of Dr. Straus's article the last two of the eleven scientists referred to above rounded out the basic anti-Huxley/Haeckel picture. They were both from Great Britain, and again, both of enormous stature.

Since 1954 an extraordinary double-barreled process has taken place: the combined opinions of these eleven men have conquered the inner sanctum of science and, at the same time, have had little or no influence in what might be termed the public marketplace.

In a process that is perhaps inevitable, one is reminded of the centuries during which Christianity completely dominated the mind of man, and while at upper Church levels certain private opinions prevailed, the masses were fed what was felt to be the most easily assimilated, most palpable fare, without any real concern as to whether it was true or false as long as it accomplished its purpose.

The views of these last two scientists:

In *Man's Ancestry—A Primer of Human Phylogeny,* W. C. Osman Hill, the Preceptor of the London Zoological Society and author of the aforementioned eight-volume standard reference work, *Primates,* endorsed the unorthodox view as follows:

> The line leading to the apes separated from that which gave rise to Man probably in the Oligocene.

That same year Professor Lord Zuckerman—who not only advised both Tories and Labourites on scientific matters during the 1960s but now serves as president of the Zoological Society of London—focused attention on the baffling paradox, a seemingly insoluble riddle, that although man started off on his own evolutionary way millions of years ago, there is not one single accepted piece of fossil evidence of his ancestry until 500,000 years ago—and with nothing really proven during those last 500,000 years.

In *Evolution as a Process,* edited by Sir Julian Huxley, A. C. Hardy, and E. B. Ford, Lord Zuckerman, a comparative anatomist as well as anthropologist and paleontologist, stated:

> Two developments seem possible. In the first place, we might expect to be able to retrace the actual morphological steps taken by man in his evolution—by, for example, the discovery of an indisputable series of "missing links" in a fossil lineage. Secondly, we might one day succeed in elucidating the circumstances in which man's actual evolution occurred. Unfortunately, both of these issues are today clouded with uncertainty. . . . As matters rest at present, no fossil Primates which would be universally regarded as belonging to the Hominidae [men or near men] have been found earlier than the middle Pleistocene [about 500,000 years ago]. . . . At the same time, fossils which are manifestly simian [monkeylike] occur in all geological formations as far back as the early Miocene [about 25 million years ago.] The apparent hiatus in man's evolutionary history between the early Miocene and the earlier part of the middle Pleistocene has so far been filled, not by the hard facts one would prefer, but mainly by speculation.

It is a hiatus that remains unfilled, and the prevailing scientific opinion is that it will probably never be filled. This despite the fact that monkeylike fossils, as Lord Zuckerman states, have been found in all geological strata from the period.

Though Dr. Leakey's statement that the Australopithecines were not part of man's ancestral tree eliminates the need for laboring this point, it is worth noting that Zuckerman's bitter, running feud with Robert Ardrey and Eugene Marais, to whom Ardrey dedicated *African Genesis,* dates back to this "Correlation" chapter, which concludes as follows:

> It is every bit as likely that some of the Australopithecines represent the forerunners of the modern gorilla and chimpanzee, as that they were the ancestors of some group of protohominids; and far more likely than that, as has been claimed, they were themselves protohominids.

Lord Zuckerman's quarrel with Ardrey and Marais centers not only around questions of comparative anatomy but also the philosophical implications involved. The back cover of the American paperback edition of *African Genesis* tells of Ardrey's "unorthodox and intriguing theory that *Homo sapiens* developed from carnivorous, predatory killer apes and that man's age-old affinity for war and weapons is the natural result of this inherited animal instinct."

A philosophical felony compounded out of structural inaccuracy, yet one that caught the fancy of millions of readers. The first time I heard of *African Genesis* was when a New York stockbroker came up at a cocktail party, eyes shining, and said it had been proved that the predatory practices of the Wall Street jungle could be traced right back to prehistoric Africa!

For the most slashing indictment of "survival of the fittest" Darwinism see the preface to *Back to Methuselah,* in which George Bernard Shaw—himself an evolutionist—states in part:

> Darwinism proclaimed that our true relation is that of competitors and combatants in a struggle for mere survival, and that every act of pity and loyalty to the old fellowship is a vain and mischievous attempt to lessen the severity of the struggle and preserve inferior varieties from the efforts of Nature to weed them out. Even in Socialist Societies which existed solely to substitute the law of fellowship for the law of competition . . . I found myself regarded as a blasphemer and an ignorant sentimentalist because whenever the Neo Darwinian doctrine was preached, there I made no attempt to conceal my intellectual contempt for its blind coarseness and shallow logic, or my natural abhorrence for its sickening inhumanity.

Though one can hardly blame Darwin for what followed in his wake ("survival of the fittest" was coined by Herbert Spencer), one only has to reread the full title of the *Origin of Species* to envision the opening of many doors, including those leading to the gas chambers.

How powerful the Ardrey-style interpretation of evolution still is, how thoroughly it has penetrated into all corners of modern life, struck home with shocking impact only a few months ago when a young partly Jewish girl who had lost several close relatives in Nazi concentration camps, but who is now cozily tucked up in the American lifeboat, exclaimed: "Every time I read about people dying in a flood or from famine in India, or Africa, or South America—not to mention an earthquake—I breathe a sigh of relief because it takes just that much pressure off us."

One might stomach such sentiments without protest if they were not built upon premises which can only be described in the light of current knowledge as science fiction. A bombshell that exploded in London in January, 1976—in the latest development in the Zuckerman versus Ardrey/Marais battle—heightens this impression.

On detailed pragmatic grounds, a four-thousand-word critique by Lord Zuckerman in the *Times Literary Supplement* ripped into shreds two books written by Marais (Ardrey described him in *African Genesis* as the "purest genius the natural sciences have seen this century").

Following the article, Penguin Books announced that they were cancelling a planned paperback edition of Marais's *My Friends the Baboons,* and that they would not republish his *The Soul of the Ape* (a title that should raise the eyebrows of scientists and theologians), as well as a third book dealing with white ants.

Though Lord Zuckerman is the object of vague, denigrating remarks in some circles, his basic position is the same as the other ten scientists discussed here. Today, however, he alone tries to stem the tide of nonfactual material.

As he points out in the passages quoted above, no proven fossil traces of man's ancestry from the Tertiary Period, prior to 500,000 years ago, have yet been found. With the elimination of Neanderthal man and Australopithecus the record since then is meager indeed. In the words of Osman Hill: "All the materials to guide us are a few fragmentary jaws, teeth, or limb-bones."

Pithecanthropus (Peking man, Java man, Heidelberg man, Solo man)—400,000–500,000 years ago—appears well on the way toward joining Neanderthal man and Australopithecus in limbo. The most formidable problem in connection with this group is that the extant fossil records show them without known ancestors and without known descendants.

The highly respected authority Sir Wilfred Le Gros Clark in 1934 tersely summed up the situation prior to their appearance:

> Of the immediate precursors of Pithecanthropus nothing is known, and it must be admitted that the paleontological record presents a serious gap here in the evolutionary record.

Nothing has been found since to fill this gap. In two equally terse sentences W. W. Fletcher, another of England's leading evolutionary specialists, describes in *Modern Man Looks at Evolution* the subsequent situation:

We now come to rather a thin period in our knowledge of the development of Man. The next 200,000 to 300,000 years are represented by only two broken skulls. [These were both found in Europe.]

Surveying five or six additional sources, we find opinion leaning in the direction that Pithecanthropus became extinct and was not in the mainstream of our ancestry.

Complicating further this already baffling picture, the bones from which Peking man was reconstructed shortly after their discovery in 1926 have been missing since 1941. As the Japanese armies were advancing on Peking, the fossils were turned over for safekeeping to the commander of the U.S. Marine garrison at the American Embassy, packed into footlockers, and prepared for shipment to the United States. Within hours Pearl Harbor was bombed, the Marines surrendered to the Japanese, and the remains of Peking man, like his descendants, simply disappeared, footlockers and all. They have never reappeared. The Chinese are convinced the Americans have them, but ex-President Ford advised one searcher: "Bring those bones to me and I'll take them to Peking myself."

The whole intriguing story was told in the Sunday *Times* (London) (November 9, 1975). Considering that no descendants of Peking man in fossilized form have ever been found, one sentence in that story warrants special mention. It refers to *Sinanthropus pekinensis,* Peking man, as the "650,000-year-old ancestor of all modern Oriental people." Thus are popular myths created, or perpetuated.

During forty-one years, from 1912 to 1953, it looked as though proof positive of man's direct evolution from an ape had been found. Piltdown man was what Thomas Huxley, the most ardent proponent of a "missing link," had confidently predicted would some day, somewhere, be discovered. It was unearthed near the Sussex hamlet of Piltdown. It was exactly what it should have been, combining unmistakable human and anthropoid characteristics. For a long time it fooled the scientific world, convincing millions of ordinary people that Darwin was in every respect right, solidly reinforcing the Huxley/ Haeckel party line.

Its acceptance as authentic for so long makes all the more remarkable the small band of iconoclasts whose work has been sketched in these pages, those who refused on structural grounds to agree that there could be "evolutionary continuity between man and ape . . . strict continuity in kind between ourselves and chimpanzees."

In the end, Piltdown man turned out to be a fraud. It had been manufactured, buried, and "discovered." Part of the skull proved to be human. The jaw was that of an orangutan. The balance had been constructed along simian lines out of white plaster and pure imagination.

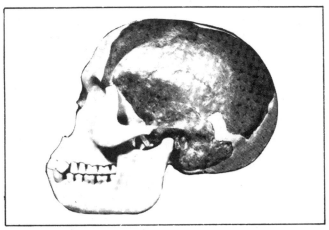

Piltdown man

Today it is impossible to hold up any fossil—fragmentary skull, jaw, tooth, or limb-bone—and declare with assurance, or without strong scientific contradiction, that it was once part of an ancestor of the human race.

The problems involved in visualizing as living creatures even those fossils that are known to be genuine are immensely complicated. Here for example are three different concepts of Zinjanthropus, or Nutcracker man, one Leakey Australopithecine find:

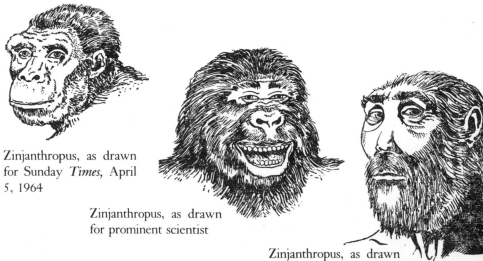

Zinjanthropus, as drawn for Sunday *Times*, April 5, 1964

Zinjanthropus, as drawn for prominent scientist

Zinjanthropus, as drawn for *National Geographic*, September 1960

And here are two of another later similar find from the Olduvai Gorge, this time with the skull as constructed by Mary Leakey immediately below:

Observer,
12 November
1972

Sunday Times,
12 November
1972

The question of whether Cro-Magnon man, who appeared suddenly out of nowhere about 30,000 B.C. in southwest France and the Iberian peninsula (his name derived from a cave near Les Eyzies in the Dordogne region) was a direct ancestor of *Homo sapiens* or should be classified as part of the human race or might have become extinct has not been scientifically determined. He was larger than present-day man, with projecting jaws, but judging from his exquisite cave art and other artifacts he was our equal in intelligence. When asked how he would do as a Harvard undergraduate, Dr. Jerome Bruner replied: "He would not be conspicuously in bad shape."

The time and place of Cro-Magnon man's appearance has led many supporters of the Lost Continent of Atlantis theory to contend that he was a survivor who fled from that disaster. The fact that there is fossil evidence he may have been negroid offers certain complications to some authorities.

The question of whether or not he was a true human is central to this entire examination. Scientists generally, but not unanimously, subscribe to the theory that *Homo sapiens* broke through only once from a lower form of life, and that all of humanity is descended from this original source. Charles Darwin himself and the Roman Catholic Church were in complete agreement on this score. Sir Wilfred Le Gros Clark, after weighing the matter at considerable length, concluded that though different origins for different races of men was a "possibility" he believed "it is perhaps not very probable."

An excellent summation of the argument in favor of a single breakthrough in terms of basic evolutionary principle is to be found in Fothergill's *Evolution and Christians:*

> In the biological sense alone a change of this kind is immense, and all evolutionary knowledge indicates that such major changes are not repeated. They occur once and for all; the conditions bringing about their further production are rarely repeated. The change which produced a creature capable of being a human being is at the very least on a par with the kind of changes which produced the various phyla, and no biologist has ever suggested that even fishes, birds, higher vertebrates, etc., let alone phyla, have been produced over and over again.

The $64,000 question, of course—in Thomas Huxley's words, "The question of questions for mankind, the problem which underlies all others, and is more deeply interesting than any other"—is exactly when, where, and how did the great breakthrough take place?

One thing is certain: There is no solid fossil evidence prior to 30,000 B.C. that it took place on this planet.

Quoting for the last time from Frederic Wood Jones:

> No skill in juggling with facts, no aptitude for simplification can weave from the tangled mass of evidence provided by the more recent discoveries in Africa and Asia a clear-cut story of the evolution of Anthropoid Ape into Man. . . .
> The pathway of progress towards assigning to Man his place

among the Anthropoids, among the Mammals, or in Nature is strewn with the litter caused by the torn-up shreds of theories based upon an imperfect knowledge of human anatomy. In this regard the position is little better in 1947 than it was in 1847.

Or today.

From conversations with people in England who knew and worked with him, Wood Jones emerges as a gentle, kindly, good-humored instructor who at the same time was as tough-minded and unflinching in his principles as any of the great scientists of history. He brought back with him from Australia, where he had been engaged in extensive field research, a wife who was part aborigine. In spite of this marriage, which was at that time a considerable social burden, he fought his way up to a position of unassailable eminence. His teachings should be required reading in the university classrooms of the world.

Reporting on today's true if often obscured consensual position regarding man's origin and ancestry is not a simple matter. Weighing all factors, the clearest brief summation is to be found in *The Concise Encyclopedia of Archaeology* published by Hawthorn Books, New York.

This reference work, edited by Leonard Cottrell, a fair-minded, objective arbiter on controversial subjects, has been republished twice since 1960— in 1970 and 1974—and a comparison of the three editions shows that evolutionary thinking stabilized during the 1950s and has not changed materially during the past fifteen years.

Working with the 1974 edition, the pertinent passages are to be found under "Primates, Prehuman Evolution of":

> It is not so very many years ago that scientists believed that the prehuman ancestors of man were creatures having many outward features in common with one or other of the living great apes of today—the gorilla, the chimpanzee, the orang-outang and the gibbon. In particular, scientists expected that prehuman ancestral stock would exhibit massive overhanging brow ridges, long arms, and that the jaws would have simian shelves (a curious ledge of bone linking the two halves of the lower jaws in apes and monkeys). . . .
> There were always a few scientists who were always a little worried by this view because, if it were true, it would mean that there had been major reversals of evolution. Everyone has long been agreed that if we go back in time beyond the stage where the great apes themselves made their appearance, we should find that the common stock of the higher primates was a monkey-like creature which had not yet developed the enormously long arms, combined with short legs, which are so marked a feature of the living great apes.

This character is linked with the peculiar manner by which apes move about and which is called "brachiating" because the long arms play such a large part in it. Those who supported the old theory felt that man, in his prehuman stage, had passed through a "brachiating" phase, and that subsequently, as he learned to stand and walk upright without the help of his arms, those forelimbs had gradually grown shorter again. . . .
Since the mid-1940s, however, new discoveries have come to light which make an alternative explanation seem more probable, and suggest *that man's prehuman ancestors may have evolved from a four-footed monkey-like stage direct to an upright stage, in which the arms are not unduly lengthened, but even shortened, without ever having passed through a brachiating stage, such as is seen in the great apes."* [Italics added.]

This single unobtrusive passage suggests that cleavage may have taken place many millions of years ago, as urged for so long by the outshouted tiny minority and vigorously opposed for so long by the noisy Huxley/Haeckel direct-continuity forces, whose hubbub continues unabated.

With consensual opinion among scientists at the top level shifting the search for man's rightful ancestry back into the remote past, the current prime choice of quite a large number of evolutionists has become Proconsul, a creature who lived in Kenya some 30 million years ago. Continuing in *The Concise Encyclopedia of Archaeology:*

His teeth proclaim him a hominid, or member of the ape and human branch of the Primates, rather than a Cercopithecoid, or member of the monkey-baboon family. But Proconsul has not got the long brachiating arms of the later great apes. He was still quadrupedal in his gait, with more or less equal length of arm and leg. He was a climbing quadruped, however, with some obvious monkey characters in his limbs, and others which foreshadow the form seen in the apes.

Assuming for the moment that Proconsul was our ancestor, there is still that vast void of about 30 million years between him and us with no sign of any connecting links. And when one takes a closer look at him, the chances of his being our great great great etc. etc. grandparent are hardly what one would describe as a sure thing—the conflicting opinions about him only emphasize how tenuous the theory of man's terrestrial evolution has become.

Proconsul is not a recent find. His fossils were discovered in the early 1930s, and how he got his name is indicative of opinions about him in those days. When his remains were shipped to London and unpacked, they resembled a chimpanzee so closely that he was named in honor of a great favorite of children visiting the London Zoo who belonged to that species and who was affectionately known as Consul.

No one at that time thought he would ever be put forward seriously as a contender in the "Great Homo Sapiens' Ancestral Sweepstakes." He has arrived where he is mainly by default, through the elimination, one by one, of candidates whose vintage is less ancient.

Here are just a few of the sources that withhold endorsement of this choice:

A. T. Hapwood, who played a key role in the Proconsul discoveries, wrote two articles in 1933 presenting substantial evidence that he was not in the line of human descent but more closely related to the chimpanzee (see Bibliography).

W. W. Fletcher, Professor of Biology and past Dean of the School of Biological Sciences, University of Strathclyde, Scotland (see *Modern Man Looks at Evolution*):

> He [Proconsul] was probably the forerunner of monkeys and apes. The question of his relationship to Man is still open.

The Observer (London, January 13, 1966):

> Whether Proconsul himself is a direct ancestor of man, or a sideline, is not settled.

Philip G. Fothergill (Evolution and Christians, 1961):

> This creature along with the two species of *Limnopithecus* and with *Xenopithecus* [both identified with A. T. Hapwood], although they are recent fossil finds, are not seriously regarded as being near to man, or intermediate between man and ape.

W. C. Osman Hill (Man's Ancestry—A Primer of Human Phylogeny):

> Clearly Proconsul represents an important evolutionary horizon in the progressive advance towards hominid structural and adaptational requirements; this does not necessarily mean that it was on the direct lineage towards Man, though it may have been ancestral to modern giant apes.

Proconsul's "youth," aside from any other factors, would have ruled him out as far as Cope, Hübrecht, Boule, Broom, and Wood Jones are concerned.

Again, regarding this major detail of the "question of questions," are we pinning our hopes on faith or fact? When we try to assemble an orderly summation out of the present confusion, three facts emerge:

1. The position as summarized in *The Concise Encyclopedia of Archaeology* indicates that it is unlikely that man evolved from any ape but broke off from the primate stem at least 25 to 30 million years ago, with a number of scientists proposing a far earlier date—60 to 80 million years ago.

2. On the strict basis of comparative anatomy, *Homo sapiens'* upright position must have been attained many millions of years ago. In the absence of reliable fossil evidence the exact time that this took place cannot be determined. The upright position in turn led to man's specialized hallmarks, especially his unique mental capacities and accomplishments.

3. Despite the acceptance of these first two facts, there is no fossil evidence of *Homo sapiens'* sojourn on this planet before 500,000 years ago. Some scientists have opted for Proconsul as a common ancestor of man and the anthropoids dating back some 30 million years, but there is a strong body of dissenting opinion on this score. There is no fossil evidence before 30,000 years ago that has been positively identified as ancestral to *Homo sapiens.* The relationship of Cro-Magnon man to the human race has not been established.

In the light of these three points, an additional fact appears self-evident. The views expressed in Stephen Jay Gould's *Natural History* article, typical of a broad spectrum of current Darwinian material, bear no relationship whatsoever to the facts summarized above, are in fact in direct opposition to them. Two different planets might be under discussion.*

Professor Gould insinuates that opposition to the acceptance of continuity between man and other primates is essentially philosophic, religious, and/or nostalgic—that we are reluctant emotionally to accept our place as part of the animal kingdom.

This has absolutely nothing whatsoever to do with the case in hand. Except for Sir Julian Huxley's passage referring to Humphrey Johnson's statement that the difference between us and the chimpanzee

---

*During the past quarter century the controversy between the orthodox, Huxley/Haeckel, "Darwinian" or "Neo-Darwinian" evolutionists and the unorthodox group has died away, apparently without the general public's being aware that it ever took place. The summation of the current scientific consensus in *The Concise Encyclopedia of Archaeology*—which has remained basically the same for nearly twenty years and which is the fairest and most objective I have been able to find—indicates that the two groups have come together but that at the same time the previous orthodox position has been drastically altered. Thus it is generally agreed today that *Homo sapiens,* because of his basic structural simplicity, could not have passed through an apelike evolutionary phase. Thus the unorthodox position has been integrated into a new orthodox position which rather than stressing continuity between man and ape, accepts that *Homo sapiens* must have broken off from the primate stem and pursued his own evolutionary track at least 25 to 30 million years ago. This is a far cry from the days when evolutionists were looking for a "missing link," a nonforged Piltdown man, between ourselves and the apes.

is greater than between a chimpanzee and a daisy, all of the data presented to date have to do with *structural* differences between man and the other primates, with no excursion into far more complex psychozoatic questions (*psychozoa* being a term suggested in 1958 by Sir Julian Huxley to describe the vast, often nebulous, area ranging all the way from instinctive reflex actions to man's possession or non-possession of a soul).

The Darwinians are in a position akin to that of the pre-Darwinian authorities. Although many of the pre-Darwinians had realized for some time that Archbishop James Ussher's laboriously arrived-at calculation that the world had been created in 4004 B.C. (let alone the pinpointing of the main event by John Lightfoot, Vice Chancellor of Cambridge University, who declared: "Man was created by the Trinity on Sunday, October 23, 4004 B.C. at nine o'clock in the morning") no longer could be justified scientifically, they allowed the date to stand because it helped materially to shore up the keystone of a Genesis Creation with which they were comfortable and that they had spent a lifetime defending.

Today there are apparent fears, undoubtedly justified, that if any serious flaw appears in the Darwinian facade, the whole edifice may collapse around their heads, as other edifices have done in the past. One cannot overemphasize the role played by that small band of intrepid men—Darwin, Lyell, John Murray the publisher, Sir Charles Hooker, the Irishman John Tyndell, and Herbert Spencer—who, well aware of what might happen * but convinced they were following the path of truth, jointly ignited the fuse that blew sky high the comfortable Victorian society in which they lived. That society was a patchwork of ignorance, hypocrisy, pomposity, and superstition, the debris of which still floats in the air around us.

This does not, however, excuse the suppression, distortion, and ignoring of new facts in order to maintain and glorify *in toto* a theory that has itself evolved into a rigid intellectual tyranny.

In order to clarify the picture as to what the public believes today

---

* Anticipating the hurricane that lay ahead, Huxley wrote to Darwin on November 23, 1859, the day before *The Origin of Species* was published: "I trust you will not allow yourself to be in any way disgusted or annoyed by the considerable abuse and misrepresentation which, unless I am greatly mistaken, is in store for you. Depend upon it you have earned the lasting gratitude of all thoughtful men. And as to the curs who will bark and yelp, you must recollect that some of your friends at any rate, are endowed with an amount of combativeness which (though you have often and justly rebuked it) may stand you in good stead. . . . I am sharpening up my claws and beak in readiness."

about *Homo sapiens'* origin and ancestry, one hundred men and one hundred women entering and leaving London's British Museum during the first week of November, 1976, were asked the single question: "Do you believe man is descended from apes?"

Both groups were divided about equally by ages, ranging from under twenty to over fifty, approximately two-thirds of those interviewed being English, the other third divided about equally between U.S. citizens and Canadians. There was no appreciable difference in answers from the three countries. Fifty-four percent replied *yes*, that they did believe man is descended from apes. Thirty-six percent said *no*, and ten percent answered *don't know*. Of the thirty-six percent who responded *no*, sixteen percent gave scientific explanations, twenty percent religious reasons.

This sixteen percent represents those who had a clear understanding of the current scientific consensus, with such replies as: "We share a common ancestry with apes"; "They evolved along parallel lines"; "They are related to us but we are not descended from them." A university professor from Texas gave an extremely lucid description of man's ancient cleavage from the primate stem prior to the anthropoid apes.

Among those who answered *no*, women gave religious rather than scientific reasons more frequently than men—thirty-nine women to thirty-one men.

Dividing the respondents into those under forty and those over forty, the following picture emerged:

	Yes	*No*	*Don't know*
Under 40	66%	22%	12%
Over 40	22%	72%	6%

The clearest understanding of the scientific consensus came from men over forty, about two-thirds of those answering *no* giving scientific explanations. All of the women over forty answering *no* gave religious reasons.

Most significant of all, among men under forty, seventy-six percent stated that they believe man is descended from apes.

This limited survey indicates that the Huxley/Haeckel line of descent is implanted far more strongly in the minds of the younger generation, especially among men, than in those of the older generation. It is not an encouraging picture as far as the facts are concerned, with the cross-section representing a better than average education level, i.e. those visiting the British Museum, or in a few instances those working there.

As we've seen, a century and a quarter ago humanity was offered only two alternatives as far as our past was concerned: the Genesis Creation or the theory of evolution. Today there are two additional possibilities: either the bulk of the evidence related to our terrestrial ancestry up until thirty thousand years ago was buried beneath the seas and oceans in Atlantean and similar catastrophes, or *Homo sapiens'* evolution may have taken place outside the earth's orbit.

When the psychozoatic evidence, certain newly discovered facts about events during the past ten thousand years, and our recently expanded knowledge of outer space are put alongside the structural data, it would appear that we should at least keep our options open.

CHAPTER

7

Our science is but a drop, our ignorance a sea.
Whatever else be certain, this at least is certain:
that the world of our present natural knowledge is enveloped
in a larger world of some sort,
of whose residual properties we at present
can frame no positive idea.

—WILLIAM JAMES at Harvard University, 1895

During the past quarter century evolutionists, specialists working in related fields, and theologians have spent an increasing amount of time—jointly and individually—probing into what might broadly be termed the metaphysical aspects of mankind, the portion of Western Judeo-Christian philosophical thought that was well nigh obliterated by the Darwinians, who, as Samuel Butler bitterly complained, "knocked the bottom out of the universe."

The initial step toward a rapprochement between religion and science came from the Vatican in 1950, perhaps surprisingly, it being the last stronghold to resist without compromise the theory of evolution.

In that year the Papacy for the first time acknowledged that such a theory existed. Although Pope Pius XII's encyclical on the subject, *Humani Generis,* was hedged about with admonitions, it was widely heralded by the evolutionists as an important victory for their cause.

The encyclical read in part:

> Thus, the Teaching of the Church leaves the doctrine of Evolution an open question, as long as it confines its speculations to the development, from other living matter

already in existence, of the human body. (That souls are immediately created by God is a view which the Catholic Church stresses.) In the present stage of scientific and theological opinion, this question may be legitimately canvassed by research, and by discussions between experts on both sides.

A warm response to this overture was not long in coming, judged by customary ecclesiastical standards. During the summer of 1958 (July 13 to September 7), as part of extensive activities marking the centenary of Charles Darwin's reading of his preliminary paper on the origin of species before the Linnaean Society, a series of eight articles entitled "The Destiny of Man" appeared in the Sunday *Times* (London).

The first and last articles were written by Thomas Huxley's grandson, Sir Julian, who stood, like Henry Fairfield Osborn and Frederic Wood Jones before him, at the peak of his profession, deeply respected and well loved not only by the world body of evolutionists but by a host of friends and colleagues in related sciences.

The other contributors were the great naturalist's grandson and namesake, Sir Charles Darwin; John W. C. Wand, Chaplain to the British Forces in World War I, at that time Bishop of London; Lord Adrian, Nobel Prizewinner for medicine in 1932, then Master of Trinity College, Cambridge University; Rebecca West, the novelist and in 1958 among the most influential feminine voices in contemporary affairs; the Rev. T. Corbishley, S.J., Master of Campion Hall, Oxford; and Sir Charles (C. P.) Snow, the novelist and scientist.

It was a carefully chosen, well-balanced group, including, in the new spirit, two theologians, one Roman Catholic, the other Protestant. What they produced collectively was worthy of their reputations, and still merits reading.

Sir Julian in his two articles set the tone and pace for the others. It would be difficult to illustrate more graphically the differences in evolutionary thinking between 1858 and 1958—specifically in terms of the uniqueness of *Homo sapiens*—than by a highlighted condensation of the opinions he expressed, views which in the main were echoed by the others.

In essence, by emphasizing the psychosocial nature of the evolutionary process as it operates today, limited to man only, in the opinion of most scientists, he invited the churchmen, who had been summarily dismissed by his grandfather and Ernst Haeckel, back to the conference table:

> Man is indeed a new and unique kind of organism and has stepped over the threshold of a quite new phase or sector of the evolutionary process. We can call it the human or psychosocial phase. Man is not just one member of one family of one order of higher mammals. He is the sole representative of a new realm or grade of being (shall we call it the Psychozoa?), equivalent in importance to all the rest of the animal kingdom. . . .
>
> Man is also unique (at least on this earth) in being now the only type of organism capable of anything big in the way of further evolution. . . . [Man's] success has filled an evolutionary vacuum, and so deprived previous dominant types of any similar opportunity. . . . It appears that in any case major evolution has come to an end except in the one direction of better brains and minds, a direction preempted by man. . . .
>
> Pre-human evolution has come up against what we may call the biological barrier. Only man has been able to cross the barrier into the new psycho-social domain. Thus man is not only the most successful latest dominant type to date, the most advanced product of evolution, but the only type capable of achieving any important advance in time to come. What he does is decisive for the world's vast future. He is the agent of the evolutionary process on this planet. . . . His destiny, it now appears, is to be the instrument of further evolution on earth.

The significance of these passages is so profound and wide ranging that a dozen books could be filled with material bearing exclusively on this single aspect of evolution—man's *uniqueness,* in terms both of what he is and of what he may become.

More accurately, many hundreds of books have been written and are still being written that in varying degrees are affected by this concept—books ranging from dissertations of a philosophical or religious nature through works on human behavior, sociology, psychiatry, and psychology, plus more technical volumes concerning the nervous system, the structure and function of the brain, and the mental processes of *Homo sapiens* as well as other species.

It is worth noting that, although on October 4, 1957, the Russians had launched *Sputnik I,* with a dog aboard, into outer space, and on January 31, 1958, the United States had followed with *Explorer I,* the only reference to the universe around us in the entire Sunday *Times* series was Huxley's parenthetical allusion: "Man is also unique (at least on this earth). . . ." Otherwise, the perspective twenty years ago was still limited exclusively to the terrestrial. (The statement on this aspect of our future that stands out from the late 1950s was made by Sir Osbert Sitwell, who predicted that the human race would devote a large, ever-increasing portion of time, energy, and intelligence to the colonizing of outer space—a prediction which today appears to have been dead on course.)

In his first article Sir Julian stated that "not unnaturally" Charles Darwin, his own grandfather, Thomas Huxley, and their followers had focused attention on man's "resemblance to other mammals, especially the apes." He continued: "Today we are increasingly concerned with his differences and peculiarities."

Two decades ago this may have been true of some scientists, including Julian Huxley, but it would hardly describe what is happening today, at least on the surface. The news media are crammed with reports of experiments that "prove" how much other primates are like us, in terms of mental powers, instincts, and behavior patterns. The advice given twenty years ago by Thomas Huxley's grandson as to the direction in which science should work has seemingly been tossed to the winds.

An excellent example is a recent British Broadcasting Corporation TV documentary entitled "The Orang-outang-Jungle Man." Brushing aside both structural and psychozoatic differences, the conclusion put forward is that, except for dwelling in trees, these apes are really our brothers under the skin—fellowmen.

And some of the work being done on communication with the chimpanzee, in sign language as well as the spoken word—comparable to research being done with the dolphin (who no one claims is closely related to us)—is fascinating but in the general context hardly appears likely to clarify man's place in the universe. Rather it seems designed, in the absence of fossil evidence, to reinforce in the popular mind the orthodox Huxley/Haeckel theory of our descent.

As we've seen, a growing number of scientists, not in the limelight or motivated by some vague, wishful desire to confirm the existence of man's soul but rather operating on the basis of hard facts, are convinced that the chasm separating us from our "earthbound cousins" is indeed as vast as described by Humphrey Johnson in 1943—that there is a "greater difference between a man and a gorilla than between a gorilla and a daisy. One is as incapable as the other of creating a civilization."

How could a creature embodying a psychozoatic system as intricate as *Homo sapiens'* have evolved on earth in the relatively short period represented by the Age of Mammals? To perform even the simpler functions of the human brain would require a computer 550 times larger than the largest operating computer ever built. It would be about the size of Madison Square Garden. Research indicates that the human brain consists of about 100 billion cells capable of absorbing one million billion individual bits of information during a lifetime. As mentioned earlier, the nervous system accompanying the human brain would have taken 300 to 400 million years to evolve.

Such facts are not denied by the orthodox Darwinians but they are frequently overlooked.

One article in the "Destiny of Man" series, aside from the two written by Sir Julian Huxley, was especially pertinent to *Homo sapiens'* place in the universe. It came from the fluid pen of Rebecca West.

Entitled "Man's Dual Nature," her contribution pointed out that ever since the beginning of history an endless throng of scientists, historians, philosophers, churchmen, and plain people had been aware of the fact that man is a unique kind of organism. Throughout the ages he had been assigned a place somewhere between the animals and the angels. It had not taken a century of preaching the theory of evolution to make humanity conscious of its singular status. Mankind had been aware of that fact as far back as one can go. Miss West cited as an example the Creation as it was described by Ovid two thousand years ago in his poem *Metamorphoses,* an immortal work in which man is placed above and apart from all the rest of the animal kingdom.

"Man's Dual Nature" read in part:

> There is a case against Sir Julian Huxley's article on "Man's Place in Nature," which is hard to state because such a statement might easily seem ungrateful to modern science in general and to one of the most gifted and benevolent of scientists in particular. But, all the same, Sir Julian, saving his presence, has based his argument on a false premise. . . .
> [He] exaggerates what Darwin and Wallace * did for the

* Sir Alfred Russel Wallace might aptly be called the "forgotten man" of evolution. His views on natural selection, almost identical to Darwin's, were presented at the same July 1, 1858, meeting of the Linnaean Society. Unlike Darwin, Huxley, and Haeckel, Wallace excluded the human brain from his overall framework.

mind of man. They did not break it to man that he belongs to a species which is "not only the most successful latest dominant type to date, the most advanced product of evolution, but the only type capable of achieving any advance in time to come." Man knew that long ago.

Rereading Sir Julian's first article in the light of what Rebecca West wrote, it would seem as though a century of research conducted by the evolutionists had led at least some of them to the discovery of a fact that had been understood by mankind since the beginning of recorded time.

Though it is the intent in these pages to limit the material to factual data, when millions of people over many centuries believe that something is true—whether that belief is true or not—the existence of the belief is in itself a fact and should be examined accordingly.

Given a comparative anatomy situation that can at best be described as murky, with a number of our foremost scientists labeling man's origin and ancestry a "puzzle," a "mystery," a "riddle"—no more clarified today than it was a century and a half ago—it hardly makes sense to dismiss as superstitious rubbish the following undeniable fact: As far back as the records go, all across the face of the globe, myths, legends, folklore, and religious beliefs have not only positioned *Homo sapiens* as unique but, going a step beyond Miss West, have related him in one way or another to various societies existing elsewhere in the universe.

Far from belonging to a creature who evolved in isolation on this planet, a being who was once a "mere tailless monkey," *Homo sapiens'* psyche is essentially what one would expect to find if he had evolved over many millions of years in outer space and then arrived here.

It could even be argued that certain "terrestrial" characteristics of man like the inbred fear of snakes and the worship of fire and the sun more logically suggest the psyche of recent arrivals than the attitudes of a species that has evolved slowly on earth. Those who have dwelt for endless generations in close proximity to danger are less likely to show extreme fear and loathing than those who have encountered it in an unexplored strange terrain.

So much has been written about the enormous accumulation of metaphysical material—much of which has been brought together in this century—that it is hardly necessary to dwell on it here. Ranging from the pantheism of the Greeks and Romans (with gods and goddesses operating on practically a daily visitation basis) to the keystone of Christianity, the descent of Jesus Christ to earth from heaven as the would-be savior of humanity, one finds on both sides of the pre-Columbian Atlantic tales of man's fall from grace, of the expulsion of man and woman from the celestial paradise (a place to which we will return if we behave properly), of Lucifer and his band of angels driven from the heavenly realms to earth, echoed in Central America by the legend of Zoutem-que and his vanquished warriors.

Such biblical stories as Christ or Moses communing on mountaintops with unknown, unearthly beings, the destruction of Sodom and Gomorrah, or events at the Tower of Babel (these latter two have been interpreted in terms of atomic power wielded by outer-space creatures) may strain one's credulity, but they make absolutely no sense in a strictly terrestrial context. Nor does such "pagan" data as the *Cumaean Prophecy,* Fourth Eclogue, Virgil: "Now a new race descends from the celestial realm." A large portion of this puzzling material would be immensely clarified if *Homo sapiens* had evolved in outer space.

One thing appears self-evident: If neither religion nor science can provide rational explanations for this part of man's inheritance, millions of people will continue, as they are doing today, to turn to less conventional sources in search of a new "bottom" for the universe to replace the one knocked out by the Darwinians.

By now it should have become clear, as explained in the first chapter, that there is no intent in these pages to challenge the accepted age of the universe, the earth, or the various ancestral estimated spans of the creatures dwelling on it. Nor is the overall theory of evolution questioned, nor man's inclusion in this lengthy process, which is, however, envisioned not on a *terrestrial* but rather on a *universal* scale.

The only point at issue is *where* did *Homo sapiens* evolve into his present unique state?

Evidence in the field of structural comparative anatomy, in the psychozoatic area, and in the huge body of metaphysical material has been briefly examined from as objective a perspective as possible, the data limited in all instances to the facts.

Coming to the very crux of the matter, over and above Rebecca West's observation that the Darwinians as represented by Sir Julian Huxley had only after a century awakened to a fact that humanity has always known, there is a second, no doubt unwitting, misrepresentation that characterizes the entire "Destiny of Man" series and which passed unnoticed by Miss West and all the contributors.

The average reader might conclude from the material that man's crossing the "biological barrier," his attaining the stature of a "new and unique kind of organism," was an event that took place quite recently. The present scientific consensus weighs heavily against such an opinion. Most scholars now agree that the capacity and capabilities of man's brain are about the same today as when he first stepped upon the stage of history.

In the absence of fossil evidence it is difficult to pinpoint the date at which this occurred. Pierre Teilhard de Chardin, the French Jesuit whose "pan-psychism" created unrest among his superiors but who had a powerful influence on both the general public and a number of scientists including Sir Julian Huxley, reasoned that man must have acquired his present intellectual powers shortly after he broke off from the primate stem. Given a cleavage that took place 60 to 80 million years ago, or 25 to 30 million years ago—with *Homo sapiens* assuming an extremely early erect posture—a conservative estimate acceptable to most scientists would be that for at least a million or more years man has been endowed with about the same brain that he has today.*

The question that naturally arises is: What was *Homo sapiens* doing on this planet during such a long period of time? Why did he wait until about ten thousand years ago before taking off, from a seemingly standing start, at such a phenomenal pace?

The two conventional reasons are, first, he was held back by the four ice ages that occurred during the past million years, and second, it was necessary for him to turn from hunting, fishing, and a nomadic life to agriculture before he could develop sociologically.

As far as the ice ages are concerned, they did not extend farther south than mid-Europe, which left huge stretches of prehistoric Africa, Asia, and South America—or comparable land masses—where he might readily have developed civilizations, not to mention turning at a far earlier date to agriculture. Our minds are conditioned to think of the prehistoric world as a gloomy wilderness, but there must have been millions of square miles on which the sun shone, rain fell, grass grew, and conditions were pretty much as they are today.

Should not a species that has explored and populated the entire face of the globe in the incredibly short span of ten thousand years, that has succeeded in reaching the moon, and which has from the beginning exhibited the same highly developed capacity to unlock so many of this planet's secrets—from the invention of the wheel to the discovery of nuclear energy—have left more traces of his previous, slowly evolving existence? The contrast between the Holocene period and pre-Holocene times becomes increasingly sharper and more inexplicable in conventional evolutionary terms.

We are dealing here with not just the qualitative aspects of

---

* In *Man: His First Million Years* (1957), Ashley Montagu states: "Recorded history is no more than six thousand years old, whereas human beings have been making history ever since they have been on this earth, a period believed to be about one million years." L. Eisman and C. Tanzer write in *Biology and Human Progress* (1958): "In the last six thousand years, man has advanced far more rapidly than he did in the million or more years of his prehistoric existence." In the absence of adequate fossil evidence all such estimates are, of course, pure conjecture. But no date less than a million years ago has been advanced.

prehistoric man, but also the quantitative. In the same 1958 series, Sir Charles Darwin, the grandson, stated:

> There is a natural time-scale in human affairs, roughly speaking a generation, and no important world-wide plan can hope to get going in a shorter time than this, and it is much more likely to take several generations. So even if we knew today how to manage the limitation [of population]—which we certainly do not—there would be little chance of getting the scheme going before the world had become so overcrowded that it would not be effective.

There is no need to point out how much more serious the situation has become during the past two decades. Those who have seen the UN documentary film *Five Minutes to Midnight* know that the alarming rate of pollution in such widely publicized areas as the Mediterranean Basin, with wholesale destruction of marine life and frequent instances of human poisoning, cannot be compared as a "survival" problem with the food situation in the "Poor Countries" of the earth. And it is estimated that by the end of this century, ninety percent of the world population will be concentrated in those unhappy lands.

Viewed dispassionately, the most fascinating aspect of what is happening to the population today is that it *is* happening. What we are witnessing is the spectacle of the accepted showpiece of terrestrial evolution—the end product of nature that supposedly evolved out of a billion-year-old process—threatening to destroy not only himself but all life on earth by suddenly, in a relative split second of time, multiplying in numbers as follows:

8000 B.C.	5,000,000	(necessarily a very rough estimate)
A.D. 1	250,000,000	(again, a rough estimate)
A.D. 1650	500,000,000	(first world census)
A.D. 1850	1,000,000,000	
A.D. 1930	2,000,000,000	
A.D. 1975	4,000,000,000	
A.D. 2000	6,500,000,000	(UN estimate)
A.D. 2050	10,000,000,000	(UN estimate based on a 75-year projection)

Neither of the stock answers for this sudden increase in the population rate is satisfactory.

Certainly, given vast tracts of pastoral and potentially arable lands in the southern hemisphere before and during the four ice ages—some areas teeming with animals, birds, and fish—the Malthusian theory of population would not account for the above pattern.

The Surrey curate and part-time Jesus College, Cambridge, scholar based his opinions on two major *postulata:* "First, that food is necessary to the existence of man. Secondly, that the passion between the sexes is necessary and will remain nearly in its present state." Neither postulate would appear to explain *Homo sapiens'* failure to multiply in significant numbers prior to 8000 B.C.

As for the improvements in medicine and hygiene, which have played a key role in the population growth since the seventeenth century, as will be seen in the next section, modern science is only now relearning much that ancient man already knew. If it had not been for his "forgetfulness" since the classical period and especially during the Dark Ages, our population dilemma today would be far worse than it is.

Is it merely a coincidence that after a dip during two millennia we find man's average life-span rising toward the traditional biblical three score years and ten? And there is some legendary evidence—Methuselah, etc.—that at an earlier date it had been considerably longer.

Both the population and life expectancy charts appear to fit more logically a species that arrived on this planet twenty or thirty thousand years ago rather than one that has been here for several million years—basically similar to modern man in structure, brain capacity, and sexual drive—or, if Teilhard de Chardin's reasoning is correct, a far greater period.

More and more it would appear that *Homo sapiens* may be caught up in some inevitable, inescapable process, one preordained by Nature—or God—that is simply not geared to narrow terrestrial resources but which in the aggregate requires the whole world as its oyster.

It is not the total number of people on earth that hurts. It is the necessities, or, more accurately, the demands of each individual as standards of living improve. Mankind instinctively seems to be in search of the good life. The more than 4 billion people on earth today could be fitted, standing up, on the island of Nantucket. It would be a tight squeeze but they would fit.

Conceivably the original primary purpose of *Homo sapiens* was to populate this globe, a purpose one sees reflected in the sanctification of prostitution in such early civilizations as the Phoenicians, Carthaginians, Romans, and other groups including the ancient Irish. The roots of the Roman Catholic Church's bitter resistance to abortion (a distaste shared by Thomas Robert Malthus) may well extend far beyond Christian times, being more instinctive and subconscious than dogmatic.

If to populate was the original objective, one can only say wryly: Well done! The objective has certainly been attained. We are obviously running head on into a perilous situation with built-in problems no political system or leader—nor scientist—can cope with, problems stemming from the dual nature of the creature and his inherent habits and requirements. We are now threatening to destroy not only ourselves but all life on earth, which, considering the endless time and trouble that culminated in the evolution of *Homo sapiens,* seems like a most unnatural state of affairs, unless there is some unsuspected dimension to our predicament.

Such a dimension was added in 1957 when the Russians launched *Sputnik I*—a curious coincidence because as this planet was becoming more and more overcrowded, the eventual departure into outer space of some inhabitants became at least a faint possibility.

With the first landing of men on the moon a decade later the new dimension became considerably more clarified. But the most significant example of coming events casting their shadows before them was contained in an Associated Press release datelined Mountain View, California, August 22, 1975.

Given the background of a deeply ingrained colonizing instinct that extends back into prehistory and covers the earth today with vestiges of colonialism—a background that bears no relationship to "territorial imperatives" or adjacent land areas—it perhaps should not have come as too much of a surprise. And yet nothing illustrates more dramatically how much *Homo sapiens'* place in the universe has changed since World War II, let alone since Thomas Huxley wrote *Man's Place in Nature.* The Associated Press release is of such pertinence to the subject at hand that it is reprinted in full:

> A $100 billion city in space that would house 10,000 people and beam solar energy to earth could be a realization within 20 years, according to a select team of scholars.
> After a 10-week study, 28 scientists, engineers and students have recommended that the United States create space

colonies using technology already available and minerals mined from the moon.

The scholars said a space colony, once built, could transmit limitless solar energy to earth 24 hours a day.

Dr. Gerald K. O'Neill, a Princeton University physics professor, originated the space colony idea. The summer-long study session was sponsored by NASA and the American Society of Engineering Education.

In an interview, O'Neill said the first hurdle proponents face is convincing the government and public that living in space is no longer a dream, but an achievable goal.

"I'd say people have been planetary chauvinists," said O'Neill. "They haven't considered living anywhere but on earth because they've believed they couldn't live anywhere else."

As envisioned, the space colony would resemble a mile-wide wheel and have 10,000 inhabitants living in the outer rim. The vessel would orbit between the earth and the moon some 280,000 miles in space.

Food for all residents would grow on 11 acres, with crops bathed in continuous sunlight. To maintain gravity similar to earth's the craft would make one complete revolution every minute.

Residents would have a half-mile-long landscaped vista and pure water would be recycled from sewage. The air would be cleaner than in any city on earth because of constant filtering.

One finds scientists from this planet seriously contemplating the building of what may prove to be the first in a series of satellites, an artificial group which could justly be called the "Moons of Earth."

Looking beyond Dr. O'Neill's project, Dr. Simon Ramo, head of Space Technology Laboratories, predicts that by A.D. 2000 millions of earth people will be living in colonies on other planets in our solar system, with Mars as the logical first choice. Dr. G. G. Quarles, chief scientist, U.S. Army Ordnance Missile Command, concurs in this view, as does Col. J. E. Ash, former head of the Armed Forces Institute of Pathology. Given what has been accomplished during the past twenty years, the possibility of eventually extending the colonizing outside our solar system cannot be ruled out.

Whether, as *Time* magazine speculates, we will get outside help is at present a complete enigma. But the greatest question of all is: Are we entering or *re*entering outer space?

Though the prospect of living in Dr. O'Neill's space colony—or for that matter anywhere else in the universe—may not be especially appetizing to some, a Gallup poll taken several years ago showing that over fifty percent of those currently residing in the British Isles would prefer to vacate suggests that at least a few of them could be considered potential interplanetary candidates.

As for those dwelling in the underdeveloped countries, it would appear that by A.D. 2000 a gigantic throng may be fighting just as eagerly for a place in the departure queue as those who on a particular day each year struggle to immerse themselves in the Ganges River to ensure that they will never again have to live on earth.

Conjectures of this nature bring us to another question lying close to the heart of the material presented in these opening chapters: Did the same process of evolution that is generally believed to have resulted on this planet in the development of *Homo sapiens* from lower forms of life over many hundreds of millions of years take place on every single one of those millions and millions, perhaps billions, of estimated inhabited planets in the universe?

Given universal laws of nature this is certainly possible. At the same time, viewed on a cosmic scale, with the earth occupying a position metaphorically akin to a molecule within a cell in the blood stream of a corporeal body, there is a stupefying element of the illogical, of the unnatural, about a system in which Nature would repeat again and again millions or billions of times, in a process of total isolation, the same laborious steps on every one of those inhabited planets.

If, as Dr. Harlow Shapley, Dr. Otto Struve, and other qualified scientists are convinced, intelligent beings on millions of planets are vastly superior to us, isn't it more logical, more natural, that a certain amount of "island hopping" has taken place during the past thousands or millions of years?

If one accepts this premise, the supplementary question arises: Into which category does the earth fit; is it a planet on which intelligent beings evolved in isolation, or is it part of an "island hopping" complex?

As to what these other intelligent beings are like, Dr. Melvin Calvin, the Nobel Prizewinning biochemist who directs the Lawrence Radiation Laboratory at the University of California, has expressed the belief that on at least a million planets in the Milky Way there are beings who are structurally and intellectually comparable to ourselves.

Dr. C. F. Powell, Dean of the Faculty of Sciences, Bristol University, England, also a Nobel Prizewinner, concurs with this opinion. Dr. Clyde Tombaugh, discoverer of the planet Pluto, is one of a number of astronomers who think the odds are strong that we will at some point encounter outer space inhabitants whom we would classify as fellow human beings.

One is tempted to offer up today's version of Buffon's dictum:

> The differences between *Homo sapiens* and all other terrestrial primates are probably far greater than the differences between *Homo sapiens* and intelligent beings living elsewhere in the universe.

When one examines in a necessarily limited space what man has accomplished on this planet during the past ten thousand years and our new relationship to the world around us, the suspicion grows that in regard to *Homo sapiens'* origin and ancestry we may have wandered into an intellectual cul de sac that in many respects is as far from the truth as the one in which mankind was trapped for nearly two thousand years prior to Darwin.

9

*As regards the specific question of human travel between
the two hemispheres, the consensual view for the past century and a half
has been that, between the arrival of the American Indians
and Eskimos from Siberia over 10,000 years ago
and the arrival of Norsemen and Spaniards from Europe
during the past millennium, there has been no significant travel
from the Old World to the New.
With increased frequency, however, evidence has been accumulating
of pre-Columbian transoceanic contact
between the supposedly isolated hemispheres.
No fewer than twenty-five Old World peoples
have been proposed as voyagers to America. . . .
In the long run, the greatest difficulty I see with the Diffusionist view
of New World civilization is not that it lacks supporting evidence,
for such evidence is abundant.
The problem is rather that, once the scientific consensus is subverted
to this extent, there seems to be no clear point at which the subversion
can be brought to a halt. From Eurasians in pre-Christian Mexico,
we are led first to pre-glacial cartography,
then to ancient aircraft, and from there to Atlantis
or the moons of Mars.
We find ourselves between the Scylla of scientific security
with intellectual imprisonment
and the Charybdis of intellectual freedom with ontological chaos.
Suggestions on possible ways out of
this apparent scholarly impasse will be solicited.*

—DR. ROGER W. WESCOTT

The above paragraphs are from a Graduate School Aquinas Seminar
lecture delivered on February 18, 1975, at Drew University, Madison,

New Jersey, by the Professor of Anthropology and Linguistics at that institution. Dr. Wescott, a graduate of Phillips Exeter Academy, Princeton, and Cambridge, devoted a considerable portion of the lecture to the book *The God-Kings and the Titans,* written by his Cambridge contemporary James Bailey.

He turns the spotlight directly on an astonishing state of affairs in the fields of prehistory and outer space, one that bears a striking similarity to the organic evolution situation as described by Frederic Wood Jones on the first page of this text.

In essence, the profound significance of Dr. Wescott's remarks is that again facts that are in themselves known to be true are rejected, ignored, or distorted because they undermine the whole prevailing concept of man's place in the universe: "Once the scientific consensus is subverted to this extent, there seems to be no clear point at which the subversion can be brought to a halt."

Thus one finds—all the way from the comparative structure of primates to outer space phenomena—the entire Darwinian structure riddled with the same "Jesuitical" sophistry and deceit. The question naturally rises: If it is necessary to employ such methods to support the basic thesis, how solid and trustworthy is that basic thesis?

Discussions and correspondence with Professor Wescott and other scientists in Europe and America indicate that the academic world is currently divided roughly, like Gaul, into three parts. On one side are the Darwinians or evolutionists, and on the other the diffusionists, with an uncommitted portion in the center which weighs any new evidence on its own merits, without worrying too much whether it supports one school of thought or the other.

Few will deny privately that in the areas touched on by the New Jersey educator a large number of incontrovertible facts and tangible artifacts have for years been swept under the carpet and are still being regularly consigned to oblivion simply because they are subversive. Since they don't fit into the orthodox picture, they have been abandoned to the iconoclasts, who are making excellent use of them, attracting millions of avid readers, far in excess of those who are exposed to more prosaic "accepted" literature.

Never has the gap between popular and scholastic data been so wide, and this gap in itself suggests that something is wrong, perhaps fatally, with Darwinian teachings. In certain instances a single artifact has aroused grave doubts in some about the validity of the orthodox position, and in the aggregate the overwhelming amount of nonconformist material is to many deeply disturbing.

Although the large majority of them believe in the theory of evolution, the diffusionists, who maintain that early man developed initially a high culture in one part of the world—most logically in the eastern Mediterranean—which was then taken out in all directions across the face of the globe, came into being, and have grown in strength mainly because of the ever-increasing tide of such material.

The Darwinians have been motivated in large part by two philosophical considerations. First, their views support the Huxley/ Haeckel version of evolution, with barbaric cavemen and bog-dwellers presented (after the original emergence of *Homo sapiens* from the ape) as the next ascending step—primitive creatures who wandered primarily by land, occasionally floating on logs and crude rafts across short stretches of water, and who then developed separate cultures in isolation from one another.

Second, while continually stressing the similarities between man and the rest of the animal kingdom, the Darwinians have at the same time emphasized the differences between the various races of mankind, a natural outgrowth from the favored races "survival of the fittest" aspect of Darwinism.

The diffusionists explain variations in cultures and civilizations as adaptations to local conditions. The Darwinians explain similarities as coincidental, resulting from the essential sameness—what has been termed the "psychic entity"—of all human beings.

The Darwinians still vigorously defend every bridgehead, all the way from "Columbus discovered America" to "No one has ever seen a flying saucer because flying saucers don't exist"—with the diffusionists drawn up around the perimeter, hammering away from every direction at what they consider is far too dogmatic and narrow a concept of man's place in the universe.

The unsuspecting scientist who discovers an iron nail in a five-hundred-year-old Andean stratum, or a central African rock carving which looks remarkably like an astronaut in a space suit, or an inscription in a New Guinea cave that closely resembles ancient Libyan or Egyptian must watch his step or he will find himself—even before exhibiting nail, carving, or inscription—swiftly consigned to the lunatic fringe.

He is in a position akin to the astronomer who observes through his telescope a large foreign body near one of the planets, or the airline pilot who sights what appears to be an unidentified flying object. If something doesn't fit into the accepted scheme of things, based on what has happened to others in the past, discretion is indeed the better part of valor.

When Dr. Cyrus H. Gordon, a courageous diffusionist front-runner, was about to discuss pre-Columbian transatlantic voyages on the Brazilian National TV network several Christmas Eves ago, and the power was blacked out a few minutes before the program was to start; or when, halfway through a series of thirty-nine taped shows dealing with UFOs that was being broadcast by the leading French radio network, the network's Paris offices were broken into at night and the remaining tapes stolen, it is difficult to say that we have truly escaped from the Dark Ages.

Whether or not ancient seafarers crossed the Atlantic and Pacific thousands of years ago, or whether or not there are such things as flying saucers are merely ancillary questions compared to the major question: Are scientists to be allowed to examine facts and artifacts objectively, free from a tyranny that at times is as rigid and uncompromising as the Inquisition?

While one can sympathize with the academic community's desire for order rather than chaos, it is impossible to go along with the processes described by Wood Jones and Wescott without sacrificing intellectual honesty. Only by following the truth no matter where it may lead, as Darwin and his followers did in their day, is there any hope of a new order emerging out of present chaos.

There are four major ways in which the Darwinians have bent the facts to fit their theory as far as prehistory and outer space are concerned:

1. The capabilities and accomplishments of early man in the Mediterranean and Asia Minor portions of the earth have been constantly denigrated.
2. An iron curtain has been erected between those areas and the rest of the world, including northern Europe and the Far East.
3. An iron curtain has been erected sealing off the Americas from ancient outside contact except via the traditional Siberian/Bering Strait/Alaskan route.
4. An iron curtain has been erected sealing off the earth from outer space in terms of any possible intrusions past or present.

What is especially disturbing is the number of times since World

War II that those whose opinions in the past were mercilessly ridiculed or totally ignored by their contemporaries have been completely vindicated by new discoveries. The most dramatic and perhaps the most significant of these recent reversals centered around the so-called Glozel "scandal" or "farce," occasionally more kindly referred to as the Glozel "mystery."

In 1924, buried in the fields of his family's farm at Glozel, near Vichy in southwest France, a number of inscribed clay tablets were discovered by sixteen-year-old Emile Fradin. For the next three years a hot controversy raged over their antiquity and authenticity. Some scientists dismissed them as unimportant, not old, and/or as out-and-out fakes. Others who examined them weren't so sure. There were equally bitter arguments over clay pottery found with the tablets.

In 1927 a worldwide body of scholars ruled that the findings were "forgeries, manufactured and buried by Fradin himself." Academicians were in the main satisfied with this verdict, although intermittently the controversy flared up again without any substantial evidence being put forward in Fradin's favor.

The factor ruling most heavily against the validity of his findings was that on some of the pottery there were drawings of reindeer and panthers. These two species had become extinct in that part of the world about the end of the last Ice Age, approximately eight thousand years before Christ, at the very beginning of the Holocene period.

Inscriptions on the tablets were in an alphabet resembling Phoenician, but if they and the pottery were nearly ten thousand years old, then writing must have been invented some four to five thousand years before the Sumerians supposedly developed this basic means of recording and communicating. Although the panel of experts agreed there were resemblances to Phoenician, the possibility that man might have been writing at the very beginning of his terrestrial wanderings was too much for them to accept. The similarities were put down to Fradin's ingenuity, a considerable feat for a relatively untutored farm boy.

Forty-five years later, in 1972, a Swedish amateur archaeologist, Sture Eilow, went to thirty-six-year-old Gavn Majdahl, a physicist on the staff of Denmark's Atomic Energy Commission's research laboratories, and urged him to reinvestigate the Glozel tablets and pottery.

Financed by Denmark's Governmental Research Council and the Atomic Energy Center, Majdahl had been working for several years on the development and application of the thermoluminescence dating method invented in Britain during the late 1960s.

Majdahl reacted favorably to Eilow's suggestion. Extensive tests were conducted on some of Fradin's "fakes." The results can only be described as sensational. The experts were wrong. Both tablets and pottery are extremely ancient, exactly how old Majdahl was not prepared to say but at least quite a few thousand years old, with the reindeer and panther drawings pointing toward an early Holocene date. Similar tests conducted at Edinburgh's National Museum of Antiquities confirmed the young Danish physicist's findings.

Fortunately, in this case, unlike so many other comparable episodes, Fradin is still alive. Said Majdahl in an Associated Press report datelined Copenhagen, August 28, 1975: "It is fascinating, of course, to perhaps help bring full rehabilitation for Emile Fradin, now 68. But Glozel just happened to provide the first dramatic demonstration of the potentials of the new technique."

Developments since August, 1975, have not been auspicious. Majdahl has been working on a scholarship at the National Museum of Antiquities. Two letters I wrote to the Director of the Museum requesting further information on the Glozel matter have met with silence.

It is perhaps unfair to suggest that Majdahl has been whisked behind a Darwinian iron curtain and that the artifacts discovered at Glozel once again will be slowly forgotten as pieces of evidence that "don't fit." And yet such has been the fate of similar findings.

In the last chapter of *Before Civilization* (1973), a powerful defense of the evolutionist position, Dr. Colin Renfrew, one of the world's most brilliant scholars, urges that the emphasis in prehistoric archaeology be shifted from "artifacts" to "societies."

But what then should be done with the tablets and pottery of Glozel? Should they—as was done so often in the early years of the Renaissance with "pagan" Etruscan, Greek, and Roman sculpture—be smashed to bits or reburied in the ground?

Two other recent discoveries in the Mediterranean region have been heralded in some quarters as calling for drastic rewritings of man's early history, and yet the records have a peculiar habit of remaining as written. (The discovery in the early 1970s of a prehistoric settlement beneath an ancient graveyard on the northwest coast of Ireland, distinguished by sophisticated cut stones, led Dr. Ian Blake of Balliol College, Oxford, archaeological columnist of the *Irish Times*, to declare that this one find would mean a "complete rewriting of prehistory" in the British Isles. To date the only development has been a TV documentary, *Ireland's First Farmers,* which snugly tucks the settlement into the accepted framework with links proposed only between Brittany and Ireland, never a mention of those sophisticated cut stones.)

In late 1974 it was announced that the copper mines of the Timna Valley in the Negev Desert, Israel, had been dated to the Minoan period, about 1400 B.C. The Sunday *Times* (London), with Peter Watson reporting from Tel Aviv in a front-page story on December 8, stated it would mean "that the entire prehistory of metal technology, so crucial to early civilization, would have to be rewritten. The workings of the mines may even explain how the Bronze Age gave way to the Iron Age."

The mines had turned out to be "so large and complex" that the archaeologists had called in a group of three mining engineers to help with the excavating. Over two hundred shafts had been explored at various levels beneath an area that covered several hundred square yards of the desert. Some vertical shafts between levels were up to fifty feet in depth, equipped with cut foot and hand holds, each shaft having its own air channel for ventilation and making possible the use of oil lamps.

Also uncovered at the site were the "remains of the earliest complete smelting plant ever discovered." Tests carried out on recovered slag at the Borax Laboratories in Chessington, Surrey, showed that "by 1200 B.C. the smelting method then used in Israel was every bit as efficient as present-day techniques in separating copper from ore."

The British-backed international team of archaeologists found that the miners, who they think were Egyptians, dug with bronze chisels, as well as stone hammers. In their opinion it would appear "to have been at Timna that the use of iron oxide to help separate copper from the ore was first tried." The fact that an iron mine was also discovered in the valley leads them to believe that "the Egyptians mined iron oxide to help smelt copper and then found out by accident how useful iron was."

What is extraordinary about the Timna Valley mines—in addition to the Iron Age link—is the sophistication and complexity of the operation. As early as 4000 B.C. metals were being extracted from ores in Mesopotamia and the Nile Valley. G. E. R. Lloyd states in *Early Greek Science: Thales to Aristotle* (1970): "The techniques of hammering, melting and casting were known before about 3000 B.C., and soon after alloys of copper were being produced, at first not by alloying two pure metals, but by melting a copper ore together with an ore containing another metal or metals, tin, antimony, arsenic, lead or zinc."

Prior to the Timna Valley discovery the most famous ancient mines were those at Lavrion near Athens. These were worked by the Myceneans at a time comparable to the Israeli complex, and were reopened and expanded by the Greeks about 500 B.C., some shafts being sunk to depths of 350 feet. Thus one finds on either side of the Mediterranean two mining operations dating to the Minoan period.

In another development of far greater potential significance, increasing immeasurably our knowledge of what early Holocene man was doing in the Mediterranean, and also buttressing the diffusionist viewpoint, details were announced in 1973 and 1974 of excavations carried on since 1967 under the supervision of Dr. Thomas Jacobsen of the University of Indiana at the Franchiti Cave on the Gulf of Argolis in southern Greece.

Two extraordinary facts have emerged from this cave, the largest in Greece (490 feet long by 130 feet wide), which has been continuously occupied during the past twenty thousand years.

First, obsidian remains have been found in strata dating to approximately 7500 B.C. which have been positively identified as coming from the island of Melos, seventy-five miles off the Greek mainland.

Along with the bones of large fish found in the same deposits, the obsidian proves that *Homo sapiens* was deep-sea sailing in the Mediterranean over nine thousand years ago, quarrying this so-called "Steel of the Stone Age" at Melos, returning it to the mainland, and fashioning it into tools and weapons—a practice that was carried on all over the earth with obsidian many thousands of years ago. Those who have cruised in the Mediterranean, especially among the Greek islands, will appreciate what this feat means in seamanship and navigational skills.

Second, artifacts and fossilized animal bones point to migratory links between southern Greece and both Spain and Asia Minor prior to 6000 B.C. What is perhaps the most important single find is one of the world's oldest wooden artifacts, comparable to early Neolithic objects unearthed in Anatolia, at Catal Hoyuk. The Turkish finds disintegrated when exposed to the air, but the Franchiti artifact has been impregnated in a preservative that should save it.

Today we are aware of a Mediterranean past that could not possibly have been conceived of by Darwin, Huxley, and Haeckel. Beginning with the excavations at Troy in 1871 and ending most recently, for the moment, with the discovery of a 2500 B.C. shipwreck off the island of Hydra in 1975, the several thousand years prior to the Greco-Roman classical period have emerged as a sporadic period of intense maritime activity and communication, at least throughout the cradle of civilization.

At the far end of the prehistoric pole the Franchiti Cave excavations indicate a seafaring era about 7500 B.C. that stretched from Spain to Turkey. Though there may have been lapses—as, for example, between the end of the Minoan civilization (1500 B.C.) and the rise of the Phoenician (about 800 B.C.)—one can expect that future discoveries will throw much light on the five millennia between 7500 B.C. and 2500 B.C.

When one considers what was accomplished in worldwide terms by European navigators, using only the power of the winds, between A.D. 1400 and 1800—four centuries as compared to some seven thousand pre-Christian years—it is impossible any longer to accept the teachings of those who with no supporting evidence insist that the ancient seafarers of the Mediterranean remained bottled up inside the Strait of Gibraltar because of some pre-Columbian fear of the unknown, a wholly imaginary state of affairs which is made ridiculous by what we have learned of their superb astronomical and mathematical knowledge and achievements.

Before we expand the spectrum from the classical portion of the world, it is worth highlighting what Darwin, Huxley, and Haeckel could not have known about ancient man in that area, facts that have accumulated during the past half century.

CHAPTER

10

---※---

Leaving astronomy and mathematics aside for the moment, let us consider a far clearer picture of other ancient extraordinary accomplishments that is now available. The early Egyptians' skill in spinning and weaving must have had its beginnings far back in prehistoric times. Preserved linen has been found in the royal tombs of Abydos, dating to c. 3000 B.C., during the First Dynasty, which contained 160 threads per inch in the warp, 120 in the weft.

Such an end product was not developed during a brief period. It is as fine as anything produced on today's most modern high-powered machinery. The greatest architecture and jewelry in Egypt date to well before 2000 B.C. Degeneration set in c. 1600 B.C.

Spanning the same gap of four or five millennia indicated by the Franchiti Cave excavations, at the 6500 B.C. site of Catal Hoyuk in Turkey magnificent pieces of woven carpet were discovered in the earliest stratum. During what more distant period did such craftsmanship have its beginnings?

At Mohenjo-Daro in the Indus Valley, the earliest of the six cities excavated has turned up the highest workmanship. Time and again in other parts of the world the first has proved to be the finest.

We've already briefly considered medicine in connection with *Homo sapiens'* longevity. Much of what has been "discovered" in the field of medicine since the start of the Renaissance has been a relearning of what was already known in early times.

Long before Lister, the Egyptians used nepenthe as an anesthetic. The Babylonians, Greeks, and Hebrews employed mandrake for the same purpose and in smaller doses as an aphrodisiac.

Much has been written about trepanning in brain operations performed thousands of years ago in Egypt, less about the fact that

Egyptians had gold fillings in their teeth and that dental abscesses were drained.

Foreshadowing Fleming, moldy bread was used as an antibiotic, applied to open wounds, and mud and excrement were mixed with other ingredients (found in natural form in the mud of the Nile) into medicines comparable to Aureomycin.

Five thousand years ago the Egyptians were already adept at family planning. A mixture of acacia spikes, honey, and dates served as a vaginal contraceptive jelly. Only recently have we discovered that a gum from the acacia spike is deadly to the male sperm.

As a preventative against excessive sunburn, especially on long caravan journeys across deserts, the ancient Egyptians chewed a root named *ami-majos*. We now know that it contains 8-methoxypsorate, which reinforces skin pigmentation against the sun's rays, and is used in several products introduced to the American market during the past twenty years.

In the treatment of the psychologically disturbed such drugs as henbane and opium were used. Behind all such medical science must have been many centuries of trial and error, of lengthy experimentation. With ninety-five percent of pre-Christian literature destroyed, it is impossible to determine how much classical knowledge was original, how much came down from earlier sources.

Since the Egyptians practiced embalming and mummification during several thousand years they undoubtedly knew far more about human anatomy than has been recorded. The fact that Alexandria was the seat of medical learning in the Greco-Roman world appears significant. One thing is certain—what was forgotten about the human body during the long hiatus preceding the Renaissance cost mankind dearly.

Alcmaeon of Croton (c. 500 B.C.) discovered that the brain, rather than the heart, as commonly believed, was the center of all sensations. He was also the first to describe the channels that connect the middle ear to the throat. Bartolomeo Eustachio "discovered" them 2100 years later; hence they are called the Eustachian tubes.

Herophilus, the "Father of Anatomy," practiced in Alexandria during the third century B.C. The *torcular Herophili,* the meeting place of the veins at the back of the neck, is named after him. He is not so well remembered for his discovery of the tubes that run from the ovaries to the womb. They are called the fallopian tubes after Gabriello Fallopio, who found them again in 1561.

Erasistratus, from the island of Keos or Zea, a pupil of Herophilus who carried on his research at Alexandria late in life and probed deeply into the psychosomatic side of medicine, is today known as the "Father of Physiology." He understood in detail both the motor and sensory nervous systems, as well as the digestive system and the action of the gastric muscles. Erasistratus also explored the cardiovascular system—heart, arteries, and veins. Some credit him with discovering the circulation of the blood two thousand years before William Harvey.

What is certain is that he evolved the basic principles of metabolism, the effect of eating on the human system, a side of medicine that was completely neglected until Santori Santorio (also known as Sanctorius), a contemporary of Harvey's, revived it three centuries ago.

In a field closely related to medicine, Theophrastus of Athens, who takes his place in history as the "Father of Botany," drew heavily in his research from earlier sources—Assyrian, Babylonian, and Egyptian. Having been left by his longtime friend Aristotle both the library and lyceum founded by that philosopher in 311 B.C., Theophrastus carried on his work at Athens for thirty-five years after his friend's exile.

His two major books, *Enquiry into Plants* and *The Causes of Plants,* erected the framework for all subsequent nomenclature, explained the relationship between the function and structure of plants, and discussed at length their geographical distribution. Again, the evidence was available to future generations but not seriously examined until the eighteenth century, when Linnaeus founded our present system of plant classification.

Today we know that the ancients possessed a profound knowledge of *Homo sapiens* and of other forms of life around them, much of which had been handed down from earlier sources. Moving toward the principles that govern the universe, we also know that in the fields of engineering and mechanics the classical Greeks inherited from much earlier societies the wedge, the lever, the wheel, the pulley-wheel, and the bow drill, which was commonly used for boring holes in everything from furniture to chariots and weapons.

The Greeks also employed a horizontal waterwheel which closely resembled modern turbines. Hero of Alexandria at the time of Christ invented what was, so far as is known, the first steam engine. It worked by jet propulsion, proving that escaping steam could provide power to drive machinery, but apparently it was never put to practical use.

When one examines the pre-Christian world's knowledge of astronomy and mathematics, it becomes obvious how dangerous to mankind can be the process of rejecting scientific data because it "doesn't fit" into overall accepted concepts. During the long centuries preceding the Renaissance many known primary truths were ignored, branded "absurd" and "ridiculous," or shamelessly distorted because they ran counter to rapidly hardening dictums.

Aristotle's conviction that the earth was the center of the universe won out because it conformed to the reigning establishment's scheme of things despite the fact that a few centuries before him Philolaos (in whose honor one of the principal craters on the moon is named) had proposed that the earth moved through space in a regular orbit along with the other planets.

Anaximander (c. 610–547 B.C.) had further declared that the "earth is round and revolved around the sun," while Aristarchus of Samos, whose life-span overlapped Aristotle's, had developed what was in essence the Copernican theory of our solar system.

Aristarchus was the first scientist in classical times to claim that the earth spun on its own axis: It "revolves in an oblique circle while at the same time it rotates about its own axis." The sphere of the stars, therefore, did not, as was generally believed, revolve around the earth every twenty-four hours. This was an optical illusion caused by the daily rotation of the earth.

Such a concept shook the whole body of Greek physics to its foundations, yet the depths of oblivion to which Aristarchus's teachings were consigned can be measured by the fact that in 1600 Giordano Bruno was burned to death at the stake in Rome's Piazza del Fiore because he had proclaimed that the "earth revolves in orbit around the sun," and that there were an "infinite number" of suns with planets revolving around them, of which many were no doubt inhabited by intelligent beings:

> No reasonable mind can assume that heavenly bodies which may be far more magnificent than ours would not bear upon them creatures similar or even superior to those upon our human earth.*

While the seventeen scientists who are working with Dr. J. Allen Hynek, Director of Northwestern University's Center for UFO Studies, all topflight scholars from leading American universities, are in

---

* Two thousand years before Bruno, Metrodorus wrote: "To consider the earth as the only populated world in infinite space is as absurd as to assert that in an entire field of millet only one grain will grow."

no imminent danger of being roasted alive, the fact that they prefer to be anonymous, "unidentified" as Professor Hynek put it, is a clear indication of how little the basic intellectual climate has changed since Bruno's time. At least not where *new* unorthodoxy is concerned.

On the second paramount question, the nature of matter, Aristotle's theory that there were four primary elements—Earth, Air, Fire, and Water—was embraced by the ruling body of theologians and scholars because it conformed to their views, despite the fact that long before Aristotle's birth the atomic theory of the universe, as we understand it today, had been fully developed.

Democritus of Abdera (c. 460–361 B.C.) and his contemporary Leucippus of Miletus are generally credited with being joint originators of the theory. Democritus, however, after some years of travel in Asia Minor, apparently transmitted earlier Phoenician views on the subject to the Greeks, while several ancient historians maintained that the Babylonians had developed the theory.

On this front, as well as numerous closely related ones, it is now clear that the classical Greco-Roman period was in itself a "Renaissance." No one has summed up the situation more succinctly than Peter Tompkins in *Secrets of the Great Pyramid (1971):*

> Recent studies of ancient Egyptian hieroglyphs and the cuneiform tablets of the Babylonians and Sumerians have established that an advanced science did flourish in the Middle East at least three thousand years before Christ, and that Pythagoras, Eratosthenes, Hipparchus and other Greeks reputed to have originated mathematics on this planet merely picked up fragments of an ancient science evolved by remote and unknown predecessors.

The origin point of another theory that has transformed the modern world as drastically as that of atomic energy is also lost in the mists of antiquity—the Roman philosopher Lucretius stated in his epic poem, *De Rerum Natura:* "There can be no center in infinity."

Here one finds embodied the principle that lies at the core of Einstein's theory of relativity. And Lucretius was only recording and passing on earlier knowledge. Five hundred years before him the Greek Heraclitus had declared: "The way up and the way down are one and the same." And Zeno of Elea had asked: "If the flying arrow is at every instant of its flight at rest in a space equal to its length, when does it move?"

All such questions were brainwashed from the minds of men during the lengthy Aristotelian dictatorship. Or if they were thought of, no one had the temerity to voice them.

Four related astronomical facts have been known to *Homo sapiens* since the dawn of history and yet it is impossible to explain any one of them within the Darwinian framework. They can be ignored but not rationalized, and apparently no one has attempted to rationalize them.

1. As other writers have mentioned, the two "moons of Mars" referred to by Roger Wescott, which are invisible to the naked eye, were first seen through a telescope in 1877 by Asaph Hall, Director of the Naval Observatory in Washington, D.C. Yet Homer wrote of them four thousand years ago in the *Iliad*. He called them the two "companions of Mars, Phobos and Deimos." And so they were named in the nineteenth century.

2. Uranus, discovered by Sir William Herschel in 1781, is, next to Neptune and Pluto, the most distant planet in our solar system. Observed through a telescope but again invisible to the naked eye, Uranus' satellites circle the planet, periodically disappearing behind it. In one of the earliest and most baffling of legends, Uranus regularly devoured his own children, and then regurgitated them.

3. Babylonian-inscribed clay cylinders which date to several thousand years before Christ refer to the "horns" of Venus. Today they are called the "phases" of Venus. Like the "children" of Uranus and "moons" of Mars they can only be seen through a telescope.

4. The constellation Scorpio has been so called as far back as the records go. It bears, however, not the slightest resemblance to a scorpion until observed through a telescope—at which point a star formation within the constellation shows up looking surprisingly like a scorpion's tail.

It is worth noting that the ancient Mayans of Central America have bestowed on the same constellation their name for scorpion. Dr. Giorgio de Santillana of M.I.T. states in *Origins of Scientific Thought* that the names of the celestial constellations "are repeated without question substantially the same from Mexico to Africa and Polynesia— and have remained with us to this date."

On two occasions prominent eighteenth-century scientists equipped with telescopes came off second best to the fifth century B.C. Greek philosopher Diogenes, who, as far as is known, had no such device rigged up on his improvised bathtub residence in the temple of the Mother of the Gods. In a dictum as celebrated as that of his contemporary Le Comte de Buffon, Antoine Laurent Lavoisier, who proved that water is a compound of hydrogen and oxygen, arbitrarily decreed: "It is impossible for stones to fall from the sky because there are no stones in the sky." But 2300 years earlier Diogenes had stated: "Meteorites move in space and frequently fall to earth."

In the second example, James Ferguson, the Scottish astronomer whose immensely popular London lectures were frequently attended by George III, wrote of the Milky Way: "It was formerly thought to be owing to a vast number of very small stars therein; but the telescope shows it to be quite otherwise." Diogenes had taught that the Milky Way "consists of very small stars huddled together," and we now know that the crusty old savant was correct, Ferguson's telescope notwithstanding.

In another early finding that had to wait a few thousand years for scientific confirmation, the Babylonian astronomer Seleucus stated that the moon's attraction affected the tide of oceans. When the sixteenth-century German astronomer Johann Kepler put forward the same theory, he was taken severely to task by the authorities. He couldn't afford to argue the point. One relative had been burned to death before his eyes and his mother spent part of her life in prison chains. Seleucus had to wait another one hundred years for an official blessing.

Back to Homeric times. The lengthy, intensive research of contemporary Greek astronomer Dr. C. S. Chassapis has established that the Orphic hymns, which date to well before 1500 B.C., prove that the Minoans had a profound understanding of the universe.

These hymns, used by the Orphics in the education of young initiates, reveal that at least a thousand years before Aristarchus the Greeks knew that the apparent rotation of the stars every twenty-four hours around the earth was actually caused by the earth revolving on its own axis. As happened during our medieval hiatus, subsequent generations simply forgot this basic fact and had to be taught, like ourselves, all over again.

Further, the Minoans were not only familiar with the seven planets in our solar system but called them by the same names used today. They were also aware that the four seasons of the year were caused by the earth's annual orbit along the ecliptic and had already divided this planet into torrid, temperate, and frigid zones.

Not by any stretch of the imagination can they be envisioned as thinking, like Aristotle, that the earth was the center of the universe, or that they were in danger of falling off into space if they ventured out into the Atlantic. They had established the equinoxes and solstices, and three thousand years or more before Columbus "proved" to an astonished Europe that the world was round, they were fully aware of the fact.

Dr. Chassapis has also established that his early ancestors employed a calendar of twelve months computed from full moon to full moon, and apparently without artificial assistance knew there were mountains on the moon. Underlying all of their knowledge was the understanding that the universe, an infinite space filled with ether, was governed by the same natural laws.

When one contemplates such thoughts emanating from such minds, the accepted "up from the bogs and out of the trees and caves" background bestowed on early man becomes severely strained. One senses many thousands of years of accumulated wisdom and knowledge behind the Minoans, and searches in vain for the "savage who delights to torture his enemies," to whom Charles Darwin said he would prefer as an ancestor "that little monkey" or "that old baboon."

Supporting Peter Tompkins's statement about ancient hieroglyphs and cuneiform tablets, G. E. R. Lloyd, Senior Tutor of King's College, Cambridge University, in *Early Greek Science: Thales to Aristotle,* points out that "extensive cuneiform texts dating from the second millennium B.C. show that the Babylonians had already achieved a remarkable mastery not only in the fields of purely arithmetical calculations, but also in algebra, particularly in the handling of quadratic equations. . . .

"Celestial omens were evidently observed and recorded from about the middle of the second millennium. One of the first such collections is that relating to the appearance and disappearance of Venus, which were recorded for several years in the reign of Ammisaduqa [c. 1600 B.C.]."

Dr. Lloyd states that "two positive conclusions can be drawn. First, the Babylonians had conducted extensive observations of a limited range of celestial phenomena long before Greek science began. And secondly, with the records they accumulated, they were in a position to predict certain phenomena."

One of the cuneiform tablets referred to sets out in tables of numbers the zigzag motion of the planets in relation to fixed stars, a phenomenon of which we have been aware for only a limited time.

Stretching back into the shadows behind the Babylonians one finds the mysterious Sumerians, about whom so little is still known. Clay tablets dating from the third millennium B.C., however, reveal a long, exhaustive background to their mathematical analysis of astronomy.* Two monumental research projects brought to the public's attention during the past several years have extended the scope of the Sumerians south of the Mediterranean across the continent of Africa.

In the *Sunday Express* (London, January 25, 1976), Robert Chapman, Science Editor of that newspaper and a vigorous searcher after the truth no matter how nonconformist it may be, reported as follows:

> For centuries the people of a remote African tribe have known about a star that astronomers did not discover until 1862.
>
> Their knowledge of the star is so detailed that American historian Robert Temple is putting forward the theory that the earth may once have been visited by intelligent beings from another planet.
>
> Mr. Temple, who is working at Warwick University, has spent eight years researching the subject and he reckons there is no other way in which the Dogon tribesmen of the Mali Republic could have obtained their information. . . .
>
> He has outlined his theory in the factual monthly journal, *The Observatory,* and next month this theory is to be published in full. The star is Sirius-B, the small invisible companion of Sirius, the Dog Star, which shines brightly in our Southern skies.
>
> According to the American's researches, the Dogon tribesmen, who base their culture and religious beliefs on the star, have accurate information about Sirius-B dating back to long before the birth of Christ. They have long known about its extreme density, its speed of rotation, and its orbital period of 56 years.
>
> They have also known that the Earth turns on its own axis, Mr. Temple says, and that this causes the apparent movement of the sun, moon, and stars.
>
> Their mythology revolves around a folk-hero called Nommo

---

* The *New York Times* (January 8, 1950) stated that "Schoolboys of the little Sumerian county seat of Shadippur about 2000 B.C. had a 'textbook' with the solution of Euclid's classic triangle problem seventeen centuries before Euclid. . . .

"It suggests that mathematics reached a stage of development about 2000 B.C. that archeologists and historians of science had never imagined possible."

who is said to have come from the Sirius system to establish an earthly society in the remote past.

Dogon priests have preserved the Sirius story in the form of mystic rites and customs handed down from generation to generation only after long and elaborate initiation ceremonies of which ordinary tribesmen are allowed to know only the fundamentals.

Some of the religious rites involve the drawing of diagrams in the sand to indicate the position of the dark Sirius-B in the sky near its visible companion, the brightly shining Dog Star.

How an isolated tribe could have learned about Sirius-B so long in advance of anyone else in the world deserves full scientific investigation, Mr. Temple says.

It merits even an attempt to listen for signals that might come over a distance of many light-years from the vicinity of Sirius.

In *The Sirius Mystery,* published later in 1975, Robert Temple set forth in exhaustive detail a number of factual pieces of evidence linking the Dogon tribe with the Sumerians as well as other early eastern Mediterranean peoples.

Such data take on additional significance when weighed against evidence of a linguistic nature which suggests that the Sumerians extended their civilization across Africa to Senegal on the Atlantic coast, directly west of the homeland of the Dogon tribe in the Mali Republic.

This evidence was presented in a report by Michael Pye in the Sunday *Times of London* (July 20, 1975):

The lost civilization of Meroe, a thousand-year African empire that was crushed into oblivion in the fourth century A.D. may be about to yield some of its best hidden secrets. Dr. J. C. Sharman, an African linguist, claims to have found a key to the Meroitic language and script which has baffled experts since it was first transcribed early this century. If Sharman's theories are right, it will at last be possible to read the texts that survive from a civilization which had a profound influence on more than two thousand years of African history.

Meroe, on the banks of the Nile, South of Aswan, seems to have been the fount of new ideas and techniques that spread through Africa. . . . Only ruins remained from a powerful empire whose trading links reached from the River Niger in the West to the Indian Ocean and the South of Europe. . . .

Meroitic experts consider that 80 words in the script can now be read—mostly the titles of gods and kings in funeral inscriptions. But until Dr. Sharman published his paper in the journal *Azania,* there was no claim to fully understand the language, or to link it with any others.

Sharman was a wartime cryptographer who helped break the Japanese submarine cypher in 1941, and later won his doctorate for the first convincing account of the system of tones in the Bemba language. After four years as a research fellow in African linguistics at the University of Nairobi he still lives there, unemployed.

He linked Meroitic with other languages, he says, in less than a day—by comparing Kanuri, a modern language he had already examined and the Meroitic script he had newly learned. "The odds against the long string of correspondence occurring by chance are impossibly high," Sharman says.

He then went on to compare ancient Meroitic with even more ancient Sumerian. "People had said Meroitic was unrelated to any other language in Africa," Sharman explains. "So the obvious place to start looking for another relative was in the only other well-documented family of languages that so far is unidentified—Sumerian. The link was so powerful it is almost uncanny. It simply shouldn't be as good as it is." Some academics feel Sharman has not yet proved his point. "He certainly feels that he's got a breakthrough," says Professor Archie Tucker, Emeritus Professor of East African Languages at the School of Oriental and African Studies in London. "Until he can produce an actual translation, we are holding our opinion. But I'm sure the ideas are worth following up— and I'm very interested."

But Sharman is convinced that his theory is sound—and that it has implications beyond reading of the Meroitic texts. The links between Meroitic and Sumerian, he says, throw new light on how far the Sumerians spread. He finds links between Sumerian and modern languages as far west in Africa as Senegal. And he speculates on links even across the Atlantic to Mayan civilization. "Even if my ideas are wrong—about Sumerian and Kanuri and Meroitic," he says, "the general shock and shake-up in refuting them should at least start new thinking."

Can one ask of any scientist a worthier point of view?

The twin hammer blows of Peter Tompkins's *Secrets of the Great Pyramid* and Gerald S. Hawkins's *Stonehenge Decoded* (1965)—backed by other recently discovered data—have, at least temporarily, mangled the iron curtain separating the Mediterranean from northern Europe.

Astro-archaeology has succeeded where traditional archaeology and other disciplines failed. Scientists unversed in astronomy and related mathematics are glancing up from the ground at the heavens, still only half aware and loath to admit that their long-defended position has been strategically bypassed by fellow scientists. Frantic efforts are being made in some quarters to repair the damage, but the weight of new evidence is so overwhelming it seems doubtful that there will be a return to the old school of thought.

The backgrounds against which the two books were published bore a striking resemblance. During the past few centuries highly qualified scholars and amateurs alike have been putting forward iconoclastic opinions on both Stonehenge and the Great Pyramid. Without exception they and their views have been mercilessly vilified, ridiculed, and/or cast into limbo. It is a pity that, unlike Emile Fradin, they are not alive to learn of their collective vindication.

Examining first the vast accumulation of material put together over twenty years and presented by Peter Tompkins and his brilliant research associate, Dr. Livio Catulli Stecchini, Harvard Ph.D.—termed by his former fellow M.I.T. professor Dr. Giorgio de Santillana the "Copernicus of the twentieth century"—the basic conclusion stands today unchallenged:

> The Great Pyramid was constructed as a highly sophisti-
> cated scientific instrument, an exact scale model of the

Northern Hemisphere by an Egyptian culture far more advanced than is generally believed to have existed. . . . The Pyramid incorporated the basic formulae of the universe, and was designed to help man orient himself in the cosmos and to apply finite measurements to time, space, and the seasons.

Above all other departed scientists, it is regrettable that Professor C. Piazzi Smyth, Royal Scottish Astronomer and a superb mathematician, is unable to read this judgment on his findings.

Typifying the brickbats hurled at him during his lifetime, Sir James Y. Simpson, an influential member of the Royal Society of Edinburgh, declared in a public address before that body: "The whole of Professor Smyth's theory about the Great Pyramid is a series of strange hallucinations, which only a few weak women believe, and perhaps a few womenly men, but no more."

After this masterful display of antifeminist logic, Sir James offered as his evidence that he had "talked about it to a great many engineers, mathematicians, and others, and found them scoffing at and despising it."

The Great Pyramid of Cheops at Giza is unique in two respects—its infinitely complex structure and its multitudinous functions. No one has been able to explain convincingly in modern engineering terms exactly how it was built. It consists of more than 2,500,000 solid blocks of granite and limestone, ranging in weight from two to seventy tons apiece.

As for its beauty, when it was covered with its original outer casing of highly polished, gleaming white limestone blocks—which were later stripped off for buildings in Cairo but which originally served a vital time-telling function—the pyramid must have been truly magnificent to behold, and its proportions are still immensely satisfying.

Some of the most pertinent statements written about its construction came from Sir Flinders Petrie, subsequently dean of English archaeologists, whose measurements were at the time accepted as more accurate than Piazzi Smyth's but which have since proved to be less reliable.

Petrie established that "the ancients had used saws with 9-foot blades, their teeth made of hard jewels, to cut the side of the coffer [in the so-called King's Chamber] out of a single solid block. To hollow it out they had used drills with fixed cutting points also made of hard jewels, probably diamond or corundum."

Petrie calculated that a two-ton pressure must have been applied to the drills to cut through the hard granite. He concluded: "Truth to tell, modern drill cores cannot hold a candle to the Egyptians. . . . Their fine work shows the mark of such tools as we have only now reinvented."

Here we are dealing with another hiatus of approximately five thousand years.

Petrie also discovered that the workmanship on the original casing stones, some of which weighed over fifteen tons, was equally remarkable. "The faces were so straight and so truly square that when the stones had been placed together the film of mortar left between them was on the average no thicker than a man's nail, or 1/50 inch over an area of 35 square feet."

He found too that the "mean variation of the casings from a straight line and a true square was only 1/100th of an inch on a length of 75 inches."

Petrie concluded: "Merely to place such stones in exact contact would be careful work, but to do so with cement in the joint seems almost impossible; it is to be compared to the finest optician's work on a scale of acres."

To Petrie the single most convincing piece of evidence that the early Egyptians were familiar with some principle or means of levitation unknown to modern science was a two-ton granite portcullis situated in a narrow passage of Kephren's pyramid (Cheops's son), also at Giza. It would have been impossible for more than seven or eight men to get at it simultaneously, yet at least fifty or sixty men would have been required for its manipulation.

When one considers the far more complicated engineering problems at Sacsahuamán and Ollantaytambo in Peru, or on Ponape Island in the South Pacific, the myriad suggestions as to how the megalith builders performed their tasks using methods known to us cannot be termed convincing.

A number of dramatic highlights emerge from the superb Tompkins/Stecchini work, which should be required reading in all university courses dealing with the early history of humanity. (As a sad commentary on how impossible it is to fit the Great Pyramid into the Darwinian concept, in *The Ascent of Man* Bronowski never mentions it.)

The conclusions from *Secrets of the Great Pyramid* are:

1. The Pyramid inch was based on the true size of the earth, with 50 such inches equal to one ten-millionth of the polar axis. In 1910 the

American geodesist John Fillmore Hayford computed this at 6,356,910 meters; the ten-millionth part equals a cubit of 635.69 millimeters, Piazzi Smyth's "sacred cubit," correct to .03 millimeter.

2. The height of the pyramid from base rock to apex is 5,819 inches. The pyramid extends 9 inches in width for every 10 inches of height. Multiplying the height by 10^9, one arrives at the figure 91,840,000, equal to the mean radius of the earth's orbit around the sun. The current figure is 92.9 million miles.

3. Of extraordinary significance, by dividing the total distance of the pyramid's base sides (9,140 x 4 or 36,560) by twice its height (5,819 x 2 or 11,638)—the standard method of calculating the relationship of a circumference to its radius—one arrives at a figure of 3.1413. The modern value of pi is 3.1415. The figure arrived at by Archimedes, the third century B.C. Greek mathematician generally credited with discovering pi's value, was 3.1428, considerably further from the true mark than the one perpetuated by the Egyptians in their colossal monument, which was well over two thousand years old when Archimedes was born.

At which point one must pause and ponder on certain remarks made in the 1880s by Dr. F. A. P. Barnard, then president of Columbia University. Barnard not only insisted that the "value of pi was a modern discovery and therefore could not have been known to the ancients," but viciously attacked Smyth for his "folly" and the builders of the Great Pyramid for the "stupidly idiotic task of heaping up a pile of massive rock a million and a half cubic yards in volume."

Further, he proclaimed that the pyramids "originated before anything like intellectual culture existed; they have been constructed without thought of scientific method, and have owed their earliest forms to accident and caprice."

4. Much of the work that followed Smyth's was accomplished by a tough-minded construction engineer from Leeds, David Davidson, who went out to Egypt with one purpose in mind: to demolish the metaphysical revelations put forward by Robert Menzies, a disciple of the Royal Scottish astronomer. After long and arduous research, Davidson himself became convinced that the Great Pyramid was "an expression of the Truth in structural form."

One of Davidson's most significant findings had to do with the number of solar years in the so-called "great year." Every day the polar axis of the earth inclines slightly to a different point in space, attaining its original position only once in every 25,827 years. By adding together the diagonal lines of the pyramid's base, Davidson obtained a figure of 25,826.6. Pages 112–13 of *Secrets of the Great Pyramid* are so pertinent to the basic thesis of this text that they are here quoted in full:

Actually the rate of procession [the time of the "Great Year"] is far from uniform, and is at present slowly increasing. According to Davidson, the Great Pyramid recognized this fact and provided a method of sums of diagonals at different levels of the monument to indicate the all-time mean, or average length of the precessional cycle.

To add to the coincidences, Morton Edgar, an ardent supporter of Davidson, who traveled to Egypt just prior to World War I and made extensive measurements and calculations, found that the perimeter of the thirty-fifth course, which is much thicker than any of the other courses, also gives a figure for the precession of the equinoxes.

Egyptologists and astonomers argued that if the Pyramid had been designed to incorporate the *pi* proportion, and its base had been designed to be 365.2422 cubits long, the chances of its diagonals being intentionally designed to mark the length of the precession would be simply astronomical.

Davidson replied that to build the Pyramid its designer must have been deeply acquainted with the workings of natural law: that before such a design caould be put into effect, the astronomical properties of the solar year would have to be reduced to a simple pyramidal expression.

Davidson claimed that—without getting into higher mathematics—it was evident that if you know the earth's distance from the sun and the length of the sidereal year in seconds, you can compute the rate at which the earth is falling towards the sun. This in turn would lead to finding the specific gravity of the earth, of the sun, of the earth and moon combined, the solar parallax, and even the speed of light.

To Davidson the mathematics of the Pyramid indicate that the former civilization was more highly skilled in the science of gravitational astronomy—and therefore in the mathematical basis of the mechanical arts and sciences—than modern civilization. It was his conclusion that it has taken man thousands of years to discover by experiment what he knew originally by a surer and simpler method. In Davidson's words: "It means that the whole empirical basis of modern civilization is a makeshift collection of hypotheses compared to the Natural Law basis of the civilization of the past."

As to why the Pyramid was built and its passages carefully secreted, Davidson surmised that the builder intended to monumentalize the science of his time for another civilization far in the future, much as we go about burying time capsules. According to Davidson, the builder knew that the faculties by which he was able to handle the formulas of natural law could atrophy in man, and that by conveying his sciences to beings of a later civilization, he might spur them to recover those powers.

It is difficult to find on this planet any evidence of the kind of lengthy cultural buildup that of necessity would have had to precede such an astounding knowledge of the universe. As one prominent British scientist expressed it a few years ago, the more that archaeologists have discovered about our past, the more it seems as though one high culture or civilization had spread out horizontally across the earth, without any signs of the type of vertical development that should have preceded it.

5. Functionally, the Great Pyramid served as an "almanac by which the length of the year including its awkward .2422 fraction of a day could be measured as accurately as with a modern telescope."

6. It served as a theodolite or surveying instrument. It is still a "compass so finely oriented that modern compasses are adjusted to it, not vice versa."

7. It was a precisely located geodetic marker, "on which the geography of the ancient world was brilliantly constructed."

8. It was used as a "celestial observatory from which maps and tables of the stellar hemisphere could be accurately drawn."

9. It served as an extremely accurate sun and moon dial.

10. It is a "scale model of the hemisphere, correctly incorporating the geographical degrees of latitude and longitude."

11. It may well prove to be the "repository of an ancient and possibly universal system of weights and measures, the model for the most sensible system of linear and temporal measurements on earth, based on the polar axis of rotation, a system first postulated in modern times a century ago by the British astronomer Sir John Herschel (Sir William's son), whose accuracy is now confirmed by the mensuration of orbiting satellites."

Fanning out from Giza, Dr. Stecchini has established that the geographic foot used by the classical Greeks, which survived in Europe up until the Middle Ages, was in fact the oldest foot in antiquity:

> It is now clear that the minute differences that appear in this foot in Persia, Greece, Mesopotamia and Egypt are due to the fact that it was computed astronomically, varying a mere fraction of a millimeter depending on the latitude at which it was measured.
>
> The facade of the Parthenon is 100 geographic feet of .3082765 meter, or 1 second of arc at the latitude of Athens, which is 37°58′. At the equator a foot is a millimeter less, or only .30715 meter; at mean latitude of Egypt, at 27°45′, it is .307795. At the latitude of the Great Pyramid it is .3079.

Although in 1921 Ludwig Borchardt, the German Egyptologist, wrote categorically in the Viennese publication *Janus* that "One must absolutely exclude the possibility that the ancients may have measured by degrees," early Egyptian texts recently deciphered by Stecchini give a figure from Behdet to Syene of 831,240 meters. The *Smithsonian Geographical Tables* give the same distance as 831,002 meters. The ancient mean length of a degree of latitude in Egypt is given as 110,832 meters, which compares with the modern estimate of 110,800 meters.

Astronomers, engineers, and mathematicians are gradually moving toward the opinion that underlying the scientific knowledge of the entire ancient world was a common system of measurement. A. E. Berriman's *Historical Metrology* (1953) has had a widespread and profound influence on this score.

Dr. Stecchini sums up his own conclusions as follows:

> All the measures of length, volume and weight of the ancient world, including those of China and India, constituted a rational and organic system, which can be reconstructed starting from a fundamental unit of length. I have not yet completed the gathering of data concerning the units of pre-Columbian America, because they are difficult to obtain, since the metrology of the American continent has received meager attention; but the figures I have succeeded in establishing so far suggest that the American units agree with those of the Old World. The units used in Europe up to the adoption of the French metric system were the ancient ones or modifications of them introduced for specific reasons. The ancient system of measures continues to be used today in the form of English measures; we find the basic units of the English system, such as the pound of 453.8 grams, used in Mesopotamia in the third millennium B.C.

Dr. Stecchini states further that the earliest weights mentioned in an archaeological report that has come to his attention are from Tepe Gawra, the Sumerian site in Iraq, which dates back to c. 5000 B.C. After extensive calculations he concluded that the weights were all fractions of the present-day English ounce avoirdupois of 28.350 grams. The odds against such similarities occurring through coincidence are astronomical.

For over two centuries prior to the publication of Gerald S. Hawkins's *Stonehenge Decoded* eminent scholars and obscure investigators alike had proposed that Stonehenge was an ancient astronomical laboratory. Such a bizarre idea was inevitably greeted with either derision or silence. How could mere barbarians have possessed the knowledge necessary for such a vast scientific project?

In 1740 Dr. William Stukeley first wrote of the most important single feature of the Wiltshire monument: "The principal line of the whole work [points toward] the northeast, whereabouts the sun rises, when the days are longest."

In 1771 Dr. John Smith carried Stukeley's astronomical hypothesis a step forward. He expressed the view that Stonehenge was some sort of "calendar," the thirty stones in one circle signifying the number of days in a month, which, multiplied by twelve months, equaled 360, the number of days in the "antient solar year."

In 1796 Henry Wansey, a home county clothier, stated: "Stonehenge stands in the best situation possible for observing the heavenly bodies, as there is an horizon nearly three miles distant on all sides. But till we know the methods by which the ancient druids calculated eclipses with so much accuracy, as Caesar mentions, we cannot explain the theoretical use of Stonehenge."

With all such opinions classified as rubbish, ninety-three years passed before a qualified astronomer closely examined the problem. In 1889 Samuel P. Langley, secretary of the Smithsonian Institution in Washington and founder of its Astrophysical Laboratory, wrote in *The New Astronomy:*

> Most great national observatories, like Greenwich and Washington, are the perfected development of that kind of astronomy of which the builders of Stonehenge represent the infancy.

Langley's views were ignored by more conventional scientists. It was not until 1966, in the foreword to *Stonehenge Decoded,* that Dr.

Hawkins, himself connected with the Smithsonian Astrophysical Observatory, Professor of Astronomy at Boston University, and a research associate of Harlow Shapley at the Harvard Observatory, clarified and expanded on Langley's comments:

> By "that kind of astronomy" he meant classical positional observation, the study of the motions rather than the structures—the "where" rather than the "what" of heavenly bodies. His "new astronomy" was what we now call astrophysics.

Approaching the problem as both astronomer and mathematician, Dr. Hawkins made an extensive, meticulous analysis of the arrangement of stones and holes at the enigmatic site, and then carefully measured all of the alignments. These findings, along with pertinent astronomical data, were then fed into an IBM computer.

Confirming the observations and speculations of earlier, much maligned investigators, the computer revealed that Stonehenge was indeed a "sophisticated and brilliantly conceived astronomical observatory, used by three different groups of people over a 400-year period beginning around 1900 B.C."

Despite a favorable news media and public reception, for a time it looked as though the name Gerald S. Hawkins was about to be added to the long list of assassinations performed by the evolutionists. Selected as hatchet man was octogenarian Professor Richard J. C. Atkinson, the world's leading archaeological authority on Stonehenge but hardly qualified to arbitrate on astronomical matters.

In 1953 Professor Atkinson had discovered on stone 53 of the inner circle, opposite the visitors' entrance, a carved hilt dagger identical to those buried in the shaft graves of Mycenae, but unknown elsewhere in Europe at that second millennium B.C. period—an artifact embarrassing to many and never explained to the satisfaction of the diffusionists.

The title of Dr. Atkinson's first article in *Antiquity* was not auspicious ("Moonshine on Stonehenge"). What followed was an extremely emotional denigration of early man and Professor Hawkins's "incredible" research methods and conclusions.

A second article, in *Nature,* again by Richard Atkinson, was even more vitriolic and unscholarly. Such adjectives as "tendentious," "arrogant," "slipshod," "unconvincing" studded the pages in lieu of any objective, scientific explanation of where and how Hawkins had gone wrong.

The situation seemed most unpromising. It appeared that Stonehenge was fated to remain veiled in obscurity when two of Britain's most powerful scientific figures, Sir Fred Hoyle, Professor of Astronomy and Experimental Philosophy at Cambridge University, and Glyn Daniel, Professor and Fellow, St. John's College, Cambridge, rallied to the side of the English-born Bostonian astronomer.

Sir Fred stated:

> Some workers have questioned whether, in an arrangement possessing so many positions, these alignments can be taken to be statistically significant. I have recently reworked all the alignments found by Hawkins. My opinion is the arrangement is not random. As Hawkins points out, some positions are especially relevant in relation to the geometrical regularities of Stonehenge, and it is these particular positions which show the main alignments.

Glyn Daniel commented a bit more cautiously on CBS TV:

> It's quite possible that people who were nonliterate could have a kind of calculating machine of this kind; and so Stonehenge wasn't laid out in a haphazard way, and therefore there is reason for those 56 points. Whether it is the reason Professor Hawkins gives or not, we don't know; but it isn't chance.

The tide began to swing in Hawkins's direction. The assassins' daggers were sheathed. *Antiquity* arranged a nondebate follow-up in which Alexander Thom, Oxford Emeritus Professor, wrote: "I am prepared to accept that Stonehenge was a solar and lunar observatory."

In the same article Professor Atkinson somewhat sheepishly said of those who designed and built Stonehenge:

> This is not to deny, of course, that they possessed a good deal of empirical knowledge of observational astronomy; for we must accept, I think, that the positions of at least the heel stone and the station stones, and indeed, the latitude of Stonehenge itself, are astronomically determined, even if we agree to differ or suspend judgment about the precise significance of the alignments involved.

The sun, rather than the moon, began to shine on Stonehenge. Later, in *Beyond Stonehenge* (1973), Gerald Hawkins concluded:

Astro-archaeology set in motion a reevaluation of the builders of Stonehenge. At one pole they were classified as "howling barbarians," "practically savages," and at the other pole, geniuses. "A veritable Newton or Einstein must have been at work." Somewhere between these extremes a level of attainment was recognized comparable to that of ancient Egypt or Mesopotamia, though in quantitative, observational concern, the Stonehengers in 2000 B.C. possessed a higher intellect, a greater understanding of cosmic order.

While those familiar with *Secrets of the Great Pyramid* might not agree with this last sentence, it has now been scientifically accepted that at least four millennia ago peoples nearly two thousand miles apart shared a common understanding of the universe equal to what we ourselves have only recently attained.

In *Before Civilization* Dr. Colin Renfrew put the official stamp of Darwinian approval on Dr. Hawkins's work when he stated that "there is no doubt now that our own Stonehenge is a solar observatory and calendrical device some 4,000 years old."

CHAPTER

12

---✳---

The references above to a "veritable Newton or Einstein" and "our own Stonehenge" point toward the two favorite secondary lines of defense set up by those diehards who are still desperately anxious to maintain the iron curtain between the Mediterranean and northern Europe, specifically between Stonehenge and the Great Pyramid.

Some maintain that Stonehenge was designed by a brilliant individual who wandered in from the Mediterranean and who also supervised the crude native rustics in the construction of an edifice whose purpose was only dimly understood and soon forgotten.

Others claim that Stonehenge evolved in glorious isolation from any outside alien influences. Both arguments serve to keep age-old northern or Aryan bloodstreams free from contaminating southern strains, strengthening the "favored races" interpretation of Darwinian evolution. Neither proposition is, however, any longer viable.

Dr. Alexander Thom, whose present emeritus professorship at Oxford was preceded by many years as head of Engineering Science at that institution, refers in *Megalithic Sites in Britain* (1967) to some ten thousand locations in those islands where astronomical alignments were set up with an accuracy of one-tenth of one percent.

In *Lost Discoveries: The Forgotten Science of the Ancient World* (1973), a storehouse brimming with invaluable data, Colin Ronan, editor of the British Astronomical Association's journal and a Fellow of the Royal Astronomical Society, writes of three-hundred-odd "computer" sites in the same region whose sophisticated functions were comparable to Stonehenge.

With many of these megalithic remains scattered through outlying islands as well as in England, Ireland, Scotland, and Wales, it seems self-evident that the builders were of a race that became an integral part of the evolving native population.

In relationship to Egypt, the most significant site in Britain is at Maeshowe near Stenness in the Orkney Islands. Bearing in mind Richard Anthony Proctor's widely accepted theory that the Great Pyramid was used as an astronomical observatory before it was finished, one finds a completed, essentially similar structure with the same primary function.*

The major portion at Maeshowe is a pyramid 27 feet high and 115 feet wide at the base, presently covered by a circular mound. In the center, facing a 54-foot-long passageway directed in telescopic fashion at a monolith 2772 feet from the entrance, is an observation chamber corbeled in the same fashion as the Grand Gallery in the Great Pyramid, with rooms comparable to the Queen's Chamber leading off from the other three sides, apparently for observers to sleep in by turns during long hours of night watching.

The interior workmanship is highly skilled with precisely finished stone blocks weighing over three tons each, fitted so tightly that it is impossible to slip a knife between them.

Of Avebury Circle about ten miles north of Stonehenge, a site ravaged by later builders, Professor Thom states:

> Its greatness does not lie in size alone but in the remarkable manner in which its arcs are built up from a basic Pythagorean triangle so that each retains an integral character, and in the exceedingly high precision only surpassed today in high-class surveying.

Professor Thom concluded after more than fifty years of exhaustive on-site research that the ancient structures were built in what he terms a megalithic yard: 2.72 feet or .829 meter. Here again, as at Giza and elsewhere in Egypt, a geometry was employed which anticipated Pythagoras by more than two thousand years.

Confirming Thom's findings and extending them over a far greater maritime region, Dr. Lyle B. Borst, Professor of Astronomy and Physics at New York State University in Buffalo, stated in *Science*

---

* In *The Great Pyramid: Observatory, Tomb, and Temple* (1883), British astronomer Proctor analyzes the work of the philosopher Proclus (fifth century A.D.), who showed that the Great Pyramid was used as an observatory before it was finished. Proctor concluded that it would have been ideal for such a purpose when it had reached the summit of the Grand Gallery. Although his views were largely ignored for half a century, in 1934 astronomer Eugene Michel Antoniadi of the Egyptian Observatory at Medûm supported them in another detailed work, *L'Astronomie égyptienne depuis les temps les plus reculés jusqu'à la fin de l'époque alexandrine.*

(September, 1969) that an examination of more than forty religious edifices—churches, temples, mosques—stretching from Norway to India confirmed that they had all been laid out in the same megalithic yard of .829 meter.

In Professor Borst's opinion, the axes of these structures, including a number of ancient Christian churches in Britain, were built on top of earlier megalithic foundations whose positions had been aligned with celestial bodies. Canterbury Cathedral, for example, he believes was aligned to the equinoctial rising of Betelgeuse, a first magnitude giant red star in the constellation Orion, about 2000 B.C. The megalithic ruins below Chartres, France's proudest cathedral, have been discussed by a number of authorities.

In many instances the megalithic builders adapted to local conditions to attain the same ends. Carnac, on the coast of Brittany, in acreage is the largest astronomical laboratory in Europe. Here the major markers are set in long radiating lines fanning out from a central point. The distance between markers is such that again extremely precise calculations could be made. To have erected a gigantic pyramid at such a latitude would have made no sense, but the arrangement at Carnac allowed observers to match many of the calculations that could be worked out in Egypt.

Megalithic structures in Europe are concentrated in coastal areas and on islands from the Mediterranean to Scandinavia. While some scholars still stoutly maintain these are indigenous to their areas, again *The Concise Encyclopedia of Archaeology* gives a fair-minded consensus: "Megaliths are found all round the coast of Western Europe, from which it may be assumed that the people responsible for them were seafarers."

With underwater archaeology moving swiftly ahead, some of the most fascinating complexes are turning up off present shorelines. One is currently being explored near Helgoland, an island in the North Sea. In 1958, on the other side of the European perimeter, gigantic walls of cut stone measuring approximately 25 x 25 feet were discovered 40 feet underwater off the Mediterranean coast of Morocco. They extend for eight or nine miles along the seabed. Other structures have been found off the island of Melos.

Perhaps the most famous huge stone blocks in the Mediterranean were those described by Homer at Tiryns in the Peloponnesus. A legend with possible historic overtones claimed they were put into place by "round-eyed giants brought from Lycia by King Proetos."

Continuing on from the Mediterranean, the worldwide megalithic picture can be interpreted in only one of two ways: (1) either, for some inexplicable reason, early man in widely separated parts of the earth suddenly and independently became addicted to quarrying and finishing, transporting, and erecting huge blocks of stone, in many cases employing surprisingly similar, highly sophisticated engineering techniques, or (2) such a practice originated in one part of the world and was carried out from this point in a number of directions, where it was frequently modified by local materials and conditions.

Highlights of the global evidence point overwhelmingly in the second direction.

The temple of Jupiter at Baalbek in eastern Lebanon has been featured in documentary films and numerous writings, not so much because of the temple but because of the far older platform on which it stands. Three stones weigh from seven hundred fifty to one thousand tons each. They are outstripped by one monstrous slab still in the quarry below the terrace, estimated at one thousand to two thousand tons, believed by many to be the largest cut stone in the world.

On the other side of the Atlantic, however, near Sacsahuamán in Peru, a massive cut block puts the one at Baalbek to shame. It lies upside down on a mountain, apparently abandoned in transit, and its weight has been calculated at twenty thousand tons.

All or most of the celebrated monoliths at Tiahuanaco high in the Peruvian Andes were quarried in the volcanic Kiappa region nearly fifty miles away, then transported over rough mountainous terrain to where they lie today.

Transport problems assume staggering, unanswerable proportions when one considers the immense red porphyry blocks, also of pre-Inca origin, found at Ollantaytambo and elsewhere in Peru. Geologists familiar with the local strata claim that in some instances these were transported over mountains and rivers for distances up to one thousand miles. Those at Ollantaytambo were somehow lifted up and fitted together with exquisite precision on top of a fifteen-hundred-foot cliff.

An equally inexplicable mystery exists in connection with the giant stone heads of the Olmecs, creators of the oldest and paradoxically the highest civilization in pre-Columbian Mexico. Weighing over forty tons each, the heads are carved out of black basalt. And the nearest basalt quarries are forty to seventy miles away, separated by swamps and heavy jungles.

Farther south, along the east coast of South America in Surinam, massive square blocks inscribed in an unknown language lie scattered indiscriminately through equally heavy jungles. No one has yet solved the twin riddles of blocks or inscriptions.

The discoveries during the 1970s of what appear to be underwater megalithic remains off Bimini and in various other West Indian locations by Dr. J. Manson Valentine of the University of Miami and the French marine archaeologist M. Dmitri Ribikoff have attracted worldwide attention as conceivable vestiges of the "Lost Continent of Atlantis," bringing a number of additional explorers into the area. Less well known are four somewhat comparable riddles near or off the eastern coast of North America.

The most famous of these is Mystery Hill outside North Salem, New Hampshire, some twenty miles from Portsmouth, the principal seaport of that state. Long the subject of speculation and partially ravaged to help build the sewers of Lawrence, Massachusetts, this megalithic complex has finally been receiving more and more serious archaeological attention.

Mystery Hill's unique nonrelationship to Indian culture and its coastal location tend to confute those who claim no transatlantic seafarers reached America prior to Columbus; at least no satisfactory alternate suggestion has been made as to how it got there. Radiocarbon testing has established a date somewhere between 1225 B.C. and 865 B.C. for some or all of the twenty-two collapsed structures that sprawl across a two-hundred-foot-high hill.

The precise fitting of the unmortared cut stones, the presence of menhirs and dolmens, plus other details, have convinced Robert Stone, director of the project for the New England Antiquities Research Association, which now owns the site, that it is closely related to megalithic remains along the southwest coast of Europe and in the Mediterranean. What appears to be an early sailing vessel from that part of the world, carved on an enormous submerged boulder in nearby Assawompset Pond, adds to—or in the minds of nonconformists helps clarify—the mystery of Mystery Hill.

Forty miles south of Mystery Hill two underwater structures have been periodically reported off Newport, Rhode Island. One is near Brenton's Point, and the best firsthand description of it came from a scuba diver, Jackson Jenks, in 1958. It was "conical in shape, 50 to 60 feet high, 40 to 50 feet in diameter, with the top about 40 feet below the surface." It was "built of quarried, uncemented stones, each as big as an office desk, with a parapet encircling the top."

The conical shape and parapet lead some investigators to believe the structure is related to the well-known prehistoric round tower in Newport, the origin of which is unknown but which has often been attributed to the Vikings. On the other hand the "quarried, uncemented stones, each as big as an office desk," are quite unlike the land tower and strike a familiar chord. One suspects an earlier ruin modified by Norsemen.

The other submerged structure just north of Newport was observed during an abnormally low tide about ten years ago and was described as an arch. Its exact location has not been determined, but an investigative project embracing the entire area has been set up by the New England Archaeological Research Association.

Since the coastline in this region has remained approximately static for over five hundred years, it would follow logically that any structure only a mile offshore and forty feet under the ocean surface would have to be of pre-Columbian origin.

Lastly in North America, the one thousand or more cut and grooved stone blocks discovered early in this century at Mechanicsburg on the Susquehanna River in Pennsylvania constitute another knotty puzzle for which no satisfactory evolutionist answer has yet been found. Each stone is inscribed with various single characters in an undeciphered language that bears no resemblance to any known North American Indian dialect.

The trail of the megalithic builders is clearly visible in a number of submerged sites along the coast of Asia discovered during the past ten years. Several of the most important are discussed by George F. Bass and Richard K. Winslow in *A History of Seafaring Based on Underwater Archaeology* (1972).

The four hundred gigantic stone statues of Easter Island are world famous, and the question of how they were quarried, transported, and erected has been much debated. Equally pertinent to this text, the first navigators who arrived at this remote dot in the South Pacific two thousand miles off the coast of Chile were already expert in cyclopean masonry, the cutting, grooving, and polishing of massive slabs which were originally used for funerary rites and in many cases now serve as platforms for the statues.

Elsewhere, widely scattered throughout the Pacific, are lesser known but relevant structures that continue in an intermittent chain from the Red Sea and Persian Gulf.

The most fascinating megalithic remains in the South Pacific are probably those on the island of Ponape in the Carolines, about halfway between the Mariana Islands and New Guinea. They have been described in detail by J. Macmillan Brown in *The Riddle of the Pacific* (1924).

The present ruins of the abandoned city of Metalanim (Nan Madol) on Ponape encompass more than eleven square miles, but the evidence indicates that a large portion of the original complex presently lies underwater. The existing structures are composed of massive, precisely cut and grooved basalt blocks, some of which weigh over twenty-five tons, transported from quarries thirty miles distant. Certain walls are forty feet high and eighteen feet wide, in some cases with parapets.

The entire city is in a sense man-made, resting on great cut stone slabs which in turn connect the various coral reefs. Mammoth breakwaters afforded protection from the open ocean and a system of canals built above the surface crisscrossed the city.

Commenting on the engineering problems involved and the manpower estimated for such an enormous venture, Brown states:

> The rafting over the reef at high tide and the hauling up of these immense blocks, many of them from five to twenty-five tons in weight, to such heights as sixty feet must have meant tens of thousands of organized labor; and it had to be housed and clothed and fed. Yet within a radius of fifteen hundred miles from this as a center there are not more than fifty thousand people today.

In Sulawesi (formerly Celebes) considerable evidence of a Bronze Age culture has been unearthed, but the most important finds to date are of a megalithic society whose chronology and origin have not been established. Artifacts include huge stone vats on whose lids rest great frogs, and pillars with carvings of other stone figures.

On such distant isolated islands as Pitcairn, Yap, and Malden, as well as in Hawaii, and in the Marquesas, other impressive megalithic remains have been discovered. On Tongo Tabu in the Friendly Islands (so named by Captain Cook) there is a mammoth stone tomb weighing 170 tons; in 1930 on Manua Levu in the Fijis a monolith of some 40 tons was discovered.

Tinian in the Marquesas and Rimitara in the Tubuai Islands—well over one thousand miles apart—are both dotted with lofty stone columns, some over seventy feet high. There are also pyramidal structures on Tinian and on San Cristobal in the Solomon Islands, which has been aptly termed a "little Egypt of the Pyramid Age." Here mastaba-like tombs (rectangular with sloping sides and a flat roof) are almost identical to those in Egypt dating to c. 2700 B.C.

With only a small portion of the Pacific explored by marine archaeologists, what may lie under water is impossible to assess. Reviewing in one's mind the evidence at Stonehenge and elsewhere in the British Isles, along the coasts and on the islands of Europe and the Mediterranean, at Giza, Tiryns and Baalbek, at the Olmec sites in Mexico, in Surinam, at Sacsahuamán, Tiahuanaco, and Ollantaytambo in Peru, in the South Pacific on Easter and Ponape islands, it seems inconceivable that individual groups of ancient men could have mastered in isolation the engineering skills exhibited at these world-girdling sites.

And yet, coming once again to the very heart of the matter, nowhere on this planet does one find evidence of an origin point where such unique knowledge could have developed: the understanding of some principle of anti-gravity, which we do not yet possess.

CHAPTER

13

Unquestionably the star player on the diffusionist team today is Dr. H. Barraclough Fell, the English-born, New Zealand-trained Professor of Invertebrate Zoology at Harvard University.

The deciphering by Professor Fell of a number of strategically located inscribed stones, as well as ancient writings on walls and roofs of caves, in the South Pacific, indicates that early Egyptians and Libyans crossed that broad expanse of water to the coast of Chile before Christ, and may well have provided an important ancestral strain in the Polynesian bloodstream.

On several occasions in 1974 and 1975 Dr. Fell's conclusions made front-page headlines all the way from Boston, Massachusetts, to Wellington, New Zealand, rapidly elevating him to an anathematic position, as far as the Darwinians are concerned, second only to such a celebrated bête noire as Thor Heyerdahl.

Much of the material on which Fell's research was conducted has long been available to scholars but almost without exception was assiduously avoided. A front-page story datelined Brisbane in the *Sunday Express* (London, January 11, 1976) not only supported the Harvard professor's findings but tossed into the laps of the evolutionists two artifacts that must remain, along with hundreds of others, *outside* their framework:

> The ancient Egyptians may have been the first people to discover Australia, beating Captain Cook by several thousand years. Giant rock carvings, resembling those found in Egypt, have been located in the desolate mountain country north of Brisbane.
> The carvings, on a boulder measuring 40 x 30 feet, were found by cattle farmer Ron Muller. They are similar to

Egyptian carvings housed in the British Museum, London.

Dr. Rex Gilroy, curator of the Natural History Museum at Mount Victoria, New South Wales—the first man to promote the theory that the ancient Egyptians landed in Australia—said:

"This adds to the theory. For there is evidence that eucalyptus oil on what appears to be a mummified kangaroo was found in the tomb of an ancient king in the Nile Valley."

To date no one has stepped forward to answer these two knotty questions: Who were the people who carved the early Egyptian-like inscriptions north of Brisbane? And how did the kangaroo, a species indigenous to Australia and adjacent islands, end up mummified in the Nile Valley?

During the spring of 1975, following productive visits with Dr. Roger Wescott at Drew University and Dr. Professor Johannes Rahder at Yale (see Acknowledgments), I arrived in Cambridge, Massachusetts, to find Harvard divided into two hostile factions. Such conservative scholars as anthropologist W. W. Howells and the late Professor Emeritus of History Samuel Eliot Morison were lined up on one side; an undaunted Dr. Fell, his staunch ally Professor Norman Totten of Bentley College, Waltham, and a number of highly qualified associates were drawn up on the other.

A steady flow of "Occasional Publications" issued by *The Epigraphic Society* from Dr. Fell's home, 6 Woodland Street, Arlington, Massachusetts 02174 (a modest subscription sent to this address entitles anyone to these engrossing bulletins), has kept the controversy raging. It is worth noting that the background to his findings is strikingly similar to a number of the recent scientific discoveries already presented in these pages. For the past one hundred years an imposing list of scientists have maintained that the ancestors of the Polynesians came from Egypt or adjacent areas in the Mediterranean. Without exception each has been either scholastically ignored or buried under a wave of abuse and ridicule by the evolutionists, whose stock argument has been: "It just couldn't have happened that way."

The following is a sample of those who believed in the Mediterranean connection:

In 1878 A. Fornander in *An Account of the Polynesian Race, Its Origin and Migrations* concluded that after some centuries moving downward from the Mediterranean, the ancestors of the Polynesians set sail from southern Arabia and headed eastward into the Pacific.

In 1886 E. Treager in *The Maori in Asia* traced the Polynesians back to India and earlier to the Mediterranean.

D. McDonald in *The Oceanic Languages: Their Grammatical Structure, Vocabulary and Origin* (1907) set forth a strong case in favor of a Semitic, eastern Mediterranean origin for the Polynesians.

S. W. Smith in *Hawaiki: The Original Home of the Maori* (1910) presented his reasons for believing that the Polynesians originated in North Africa and migrated to the South Pacific from India.

W. J. Perry expounded the theory that the Polynesians came from Egypt in *The Origin of Oceanic Culture* (1923), and that same year E. Best in *The Origin of the Maori* covered in detail the various migratory theories that traced the Polynesians back to Egypt and Babylonia via Southeast Asia.

Also in 1923, A. C. Haddon expounded his views on why the Polynesians appear related to a megalithic culture of sun-worshipers *(Migrations of Peoples in the South-west Pacific)*: "This civilization can be traced to Indonesia, but it did not originate there, and evidence has been adduced to show that we may look to Ancient Egypt for its ultimate origin."

Three English scholars in the 1920s—H. J. Massingham, Gerald Massey, who compiled an Egyptian/Maori glossary running to several hundred words, and Sir Grafton Elliot Smith—enjoyed such towering reputations that their mutual opinion that the Polynesians had come from Egypt was not seriously attacked until they were dead, but they too have since been banished to outer darkness by the evolutionists.

Smith's *Migrations of Early Culture* has come in for especially vicious treatment, being described some years ago by the same Glyn Daniel who came to Gerald Hawkins's defense as "academic rubbish." And yet in one key paragraph Smith outlined a migratory route that appears to be confirmed by Dr. Fell's artifacts:

> Practices such as mummification and megalith building present so many peculiar and distinctive features that no hypothesis of independent evolution can seriously be entertained in explanation of their geographical distribution. They must be regarded as evidence of the diffusion of information, and the migration of the bearers of it, from somewhere in the neighbourhood of the east Mediterranean, step by step out into Polynesia and even perhaps beyond the Pacific to the American littoral.

Students approaching the question of South Pacific origins are today advised by the conformists that all of the above should be consigned to the wastebasket. And yet searching through a sea of evolutionist literature on the subject, one fails to find any solid, factual evidence that ancient man, having wandered into the South Pacific, developed from a barbaric start—*with no significant outside influences until the last few centuries*—an independent culture or group of related cultures.

Though one hesitates, as did Rebecca West in regard to Sir Julian Huxley, to attack such a gifted and extremely gracious scholar as W. W. "Bill" Howells, son of William Dean Howells, one cannot overlook the following passage on page two of his engrossing volume *The Pacific Islanders* (1973):

> The curiosity [about the Pacific past] has always been there. Early scholars satisfied the pangs with such conjecturing as their scholarship allowed: listening to myths, classifying people into races and so on. Much of this came out of their own minds, casting about to make connections with other parts of the world. Some of it sounds rather lunatic now, the kind of "scholarship" or non-science which projects a hypothesis of what might have happened, and looks everywhere for facts, however questionable, which might support it.

A statement of this sort, in the majority of cases, will accomplish its obvious purpose. It is "anesthetic"; it stultifies curiosity and discourages youthful seekers after the truth from straying off the straight and narrow conformist path into "lunatic" areas.

Just as Thomas Huxley and Ernst Haeckel led the public into thinking that the final stages in *Homo sapiens'* evolution had been scientifically proven, so the above quoted paragraph implies that the prehistory and early history of mankind in the Pacific has been scientifically settled once and for all. Fortunately there are those like Barry Fell who have insisted on finding out for themselves.

Most of the inscriptions deciphered by Professor Fell apparently date from 500 B.C. to about A.D. 300, but there is an unsolved riddle involving the Indus Valley (the eighteen-hundred-mile Indus rises in the Himalayas and empties into the Arabian Sea) and Easter Island. The riddle is seen in the two sets of hieroglyphs on the following page; both have to date remained undecipherable. The one at the top is from the great ruined cities of Harappa and Mohenjo-Daro in the Indus Valley, which are believed to have flourished between 4000 and 5000 B.C.

The one at the bottom is of hieroglyphs found carved on rocks and

INDUS VALLEY: ∪ ∪ ∪ ⊘ ⊗ ⊗ ⊗ 8 ⊟ [glyphs]

EASTER ISLAND: ∪ ∪ ∪ ⊘ ⊗ ⊗ 8 ⊟ [glyphs]

also on the so-called wooden rongo-rongo boards of Easter Island; Easter Island conceivably dates to c. 4500 B.C.

The factor of coincidence is strained beyond the breaking point. When and if these two sets of hieroglyphs are decoded by a Dr. Fell or a Dr. Sharman, a fascinating ancient link between the South Pacific and the Indus Valley should be firmly established.

The first shot heard round the world featuring Dr. Fell's research was triggered in November, 1974, by an article that appeared in the *Harvard Gazette*. Further, its significance is highlighted in two New Zealand newspaper stories of late November as well as one from Boston in December:

On December 23, 1974, staff reporter Robert Cooke wrote in the *Boston Globe:*

> Tropic island villages, grass skirts and the hula aren't usually associated with pyramids, mummies and hidden desert tombs, but new evidence shows they may have sprung from the same ancient culture, a Harvard University scientist reports.
>
> According to H. Barraclough Fell . . . there's strong evidence to show that a six-ship expedition of skilled Libyan seamen left Egypt in the third century B.C., sailing east through the Red Sea. Their descendants now populate the Polynesian islands. Fell's research . . . indicates that the expedition visited New Guinea in November, 232 B.C., stopped later at Fiji and Pitcairn islands, then sailed on to the west coast of South America, landing near Santiago, Chile, in August, 231 B.C.
>
> "The basic goal," Fell said, "was circumnavigation of the globe, but they were blocked by the American continent, so they sailed west again toward the Polynesian islands. But they never made it back to Egypt."
>
> Much of Fell's evidence comes from ancient writings found in caves, he said, "and the records are very clearly written. The detailed records are on cave walls and roofs where these early voyagers stayed for short periods of time."
>
> The inscriptions found in a cave in New Guinea, "which is now known as West Irian, are on limestone," Fell said. "This means that during the centuries since they were written there has been a gradual seepage of water that has covered the

inscriptions with a thin, transparent, protective layer of lime. That's why they're so well preserved. . . ."

Fell's research began when he joined Harvard in 1964, where he used the resources of the Widener Library for linguistic research, comparing ancient Polynesian signs to the corresponding sounds in other languages found around the Pacific.

"The signs showed a distinct similarity to those formerly used in ancient Egypt, and the sound frequencies of modern Polynesian tongues showed a corresponding match."

More evidence, he said, came from ancient tombstones in Libya, which contained inscriptions written in Latin and an unknown tongue.

"I recognized the unknown script," Fell said, "as being the same as that of Polynesia and, when the sound values were ascribed to the letters, the resultant text read almost identically to that of Latin.

"So now we had the Rosetta Stone we needed. It was clear that the Polynesian people had once lived in Libya and were the people who the Greeks called Mauri. . . ."

One of the strongest pieces of evidence [for the six-ship Libyan expedition], Fell said, came from the inscriptions in the New Guinea cave. These included a series of astronomical maps and mathematical calculations. The discovery had been made in 1937 by members of a German expedition.

Fell contends these writings were done by the original Libyan explorers, including one named Maui, the navigator. This, Fell added, tells of a solar eclipse that occurred in November, 232 B.C. A check with the Center for Astrophysics in Cambridge showed that an eclipse would have been seen in New Guinea on November 19 of that year.

Fell said the German research expedition also turned up hundreds of other drawings showing the travelers' daily life, their vessels, fishing equipment, navigation tools and other gear. One other inscription, Fell said, is a famous calculation by the Libyan astronomer, Eratosthenes, which was used to determine the Earth's size.

Another piece of evidence came from inscriptions near Santiago, Chile.

"The newest piece of evidence we have was contributed by Professor George Carter, who found the inscription as it had been recorded in the 1870s by a German explorer. It was in a little-known journal, of which there's a copy at Johns Hopkins University."

Fell said that Carter, who has long been interested in unexplained inscriptions found in the Americas, "was reading my publications (those issued by the *Epigraphic Society*) and noticed the similarity between the writings. He got in touch with me, and sure enough, this turned out to be the one inscription we were waiting to get."

This inscription, too, appears to have been written by the navigator, Maui, and was dated in 231 B.C.

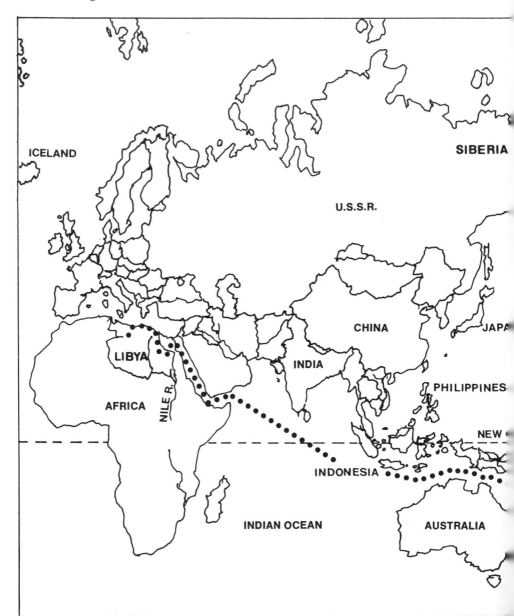

Thus a whole chain of dated inscriptions stretching across the South Pacific to Chile tends to confirm the "lunatic" views of Sir Grafton Elliot Smith and other early scholars who spent their time "casting about to make connections with other parts of the world."

The two New Zealand newspaper accounts provide additional pertinent data about the Libyan expedition and broaden considerably

Map accompanying front-page story in the *Boston Globe*, December 23, 1974. Dotted line shows route believed taken to South America by Libyan sailors.

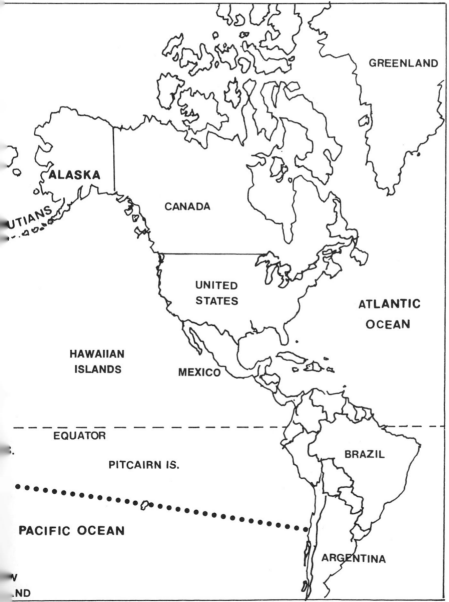

the scope of Dr. Fell's research over the past ten years.

The *Otago Daily Times* carried a front-page story on November 15, 1974, by a NZPA (New Zealand Press Association) staff correspondent in New York, headlined "Maoris Descendants of Egyptian Sailors." Tucked alongside was another article in which the president of the New Zealand Polynesian Society labeled the Fell thesis "preposterous." Not having had the benefit of seeing the Harvard scientist's actual research, this defender of the evolutionist faith limited his rebuttal to the not too scholarly argument that "this sort of thing has come up before."

The Fell article explains that the findings of the German research team at the West Irian cave had been translated into English in 1957 and had come up for review at Harvard early in 1974.*

Writings on the cave walls stated that Ptolemy III of Egypt and his Greek-Libyan wife, Queen Berenike II, had backed the expedition and that Eratosthenes, who was headquartered in Alexandria during the third century B.C., had provided specific navigational instructions prior to the voyage.

Also inscribed on the walls were "maps detailing the coasts of the Sinai Peninsula, Red Sea, Arabian Gulf, Persian Gulf, Pakistan, India, Ceylon, Bangladesh, and Burma before moving down to Malaya and Cambodia. A piece of Somalia was also drawn."

From other sketches duplicates were being constructed of sophisticated astronomical equipment by which latitudes and longitudes could be calculated. (One of these was near completion when I was with Professor Norman Totten in the spring of 1975.)

Of special local interest, "Professor Fell had previously informed historians at the National Museum in Wellington of part of his research which disclosed that a giant stone found in Taranaki (N.Z.) with undeciphered script on it had been analyzed to reveal that the hieroglyphics were a mixture of Libyan and Egyptian."

A second PA report from New Plymouth stated:

> Taranaki had quite a number of carved stones, some of them bearing marks which could be described as hieroglyphics, a former director of the Taranaki Museum in New Plymouth, Mr. Rigby Allan, said yesterday.
> Mr. Allan said carved stones were fairly unusual in New

---

* The German scientists were from Johann Wolfgang von Goethe University in Frankfort on the Main and their work was carried out during 1937 and 1938. It has taken forty years for their findings to be given proper attention.

Zealand, but more had been found in Taranaki, particularly the coastal area, than anywhere else in the country. . . .
Mr. Allan could not say why ancient Maoris wrote on the stones, but suggested they could be spirit stones of religious significance and perhaps boundary stones between sub-tribes.
Mr. Allan said Professor Fell's theories were not new in New Zealand.
Quite a number of Maoris had talked about lost tribes of Israel for many years.
While attending Maori ceremonies in Taranaki, he had heard considerable talk among the Maori people on this subject. Some Maoris living along the Taranaki coast actually claimed they were descended from these lost tribes. . . .

The Taranaki stone that Dr. Fell had deciphered from a copy of the hieroglyphs sent to him by a researcher in Hawaii (Ruth K. Hanner), is believed now to be set in concrete in Polono Park, about fifteen miles south of New Plymouth. On ceremonial occasions the Maori dress it in tribal coats.

Whether the expedition spotlighted by Professor Fell was an isolated voyage or one of many expeditions into the Pacific over thousands of years is a moot question. Dr. Rex Gilroy's evidence from Australia and the inscribed stones of Taranaki, New Zealand, both off the Libyan course; the Indus Valley/Easter Island hieroglyphs, which may establish a fifth millennium B.C. link; the geographic spread of inscriptions discussed in the *Epigraphic Society's* bulletins (through such places as Java, Sulawesi, Hawaii, Sumatra, Tonga, etc.) suggest that the curtain may only now be rising on the discovery of more artifacts that will confirm extensive interhemispheric travel over several millennia between the Mediterranean and the Pacific.

It seems plausible that Eratosthenes was picking up a long-lost thread (the gap between the Minoan and classical Greco-Roman eras in the Mediterranean region) when he championed the third century B.C. Libyan expedition.

Secrets of the Great Pyramid reports: "Current scholarship keeps repeating that the circumference of the earth was first measured by Eratosthenes, the Greek who was put in charge of the library at Alexandria, but it is clear that Eratosthenes merely cited old Egyptian information about the circumference of the earth without really understanding it." Five additional examples are discussed where Eratosthenes obviously borrowed, in some cases incorrectly, from knowledge which predated his time by some three thousand years.

On April 17, 1975, the curtain rose still further—this time in the quiet coastal town of Bourne, Cape Cod Bay, between Newport (Rhode Island) and Mystery Hill (New Hampshire).

Once again, in the eyes of the Darwinians, Dr. Fell proved himself an out-and-out anarchist. A United Press International (UPI) release stated:

> A Harvard University linguist believes he has uncovered evidence proving a Phoenician seafarer-king named Hanno traveled along the Atlantic coast of North America more than 400 years before the birth of Christ.
> Professor Barry Fell translated his latest bit of evidence from an ancient, inscribed stone on display at a historical society here. It is similar to a number of other stones found along the Atlantic coast, he said.
> Fell and James Whittall, chief archaeologist for the Early Sites Research Society of Danielson, Connecticut, viewed and photographed the stone, which was found by New England settlers in 1658 and used as a door-step at an Indian Mission.
> The stone, measuring 45 inches by 5 inches by 15 inches, bears inscriptions that had always been assumed to be Norse, but untranslatable.
> After delivering a speech at the Woods Hole Oceanographic Institute Monday, Fell returned home and worked through the night on the inscriptions. When he was through at 4 A.M. Tuesday, he was so excited he called Whittall.
> Fell's translation of the two inscriptions: "Proclamation of annexation. Do not deface. Hanno of this takes possession."
> Fell said he believed the last sentence meant, "Hanno takes possession of this place."
> According to general references, Hanno was a Phoenician seafarer who explored and colonized the west coast of Africa early in the fifth century B.C. He founded seven cities and a trading post along the African coast, and probably reached as far south as present day Gambia or Sierra Leone.
> An account of his voyage, written in the temple of Baal of Carthage, survives in a Greek manuscript dating back to the tenth century. Scholars consider it a translation from the ancient Punic tongue.
> Fell said the inscription on the stone is one more of the same series, evidently belonging to a second voyage that Hanno made of which the original Greek account has been lost. But the Greeks remembered that he did make such a voyage, that is to say they remembered that he had circumnavigated the northern ocean.

"This [stone] comes from that voyage, which, according to our Greek sources, dates from approximately 480 or 475 B.C. They report him as a navigator from Carthage, but the rather numerous inscriptions we have now found suggest to us he was not only a navigator but rather a King of Southern Spain, with his principal port Cadiz.

"He departed from Cadiz and presumably returned there," Fell said. "There's a lot of evidence and we're only just beginning to tap it now."

Fell said the inscriptions were written in a southern Iberian alphabet.

"In this particular case, the alphabet used on this stone is one called South Iberian, and it was deciphered by Spanish scientists," he said. "So it's not just a case of one crackpot Harvard professor alleging that it's this. I have plenty of authorities to support me."

With the publication of Dr. Fell's *America B.C.* in January, 1977, the veil has been lifted on a substantial number of ancient inscriptions found in various parts of North America that have long defied interpretation and/or been brushed aside by the traditionalists as "folderol." *

Out of this ever-swelling data the Harvard biologist has reconstructed a fascinating picture of pre-Columbian migrations and influences in the New World which, in spite of the usual highly emotional opposition, is so meticulously documented it will be hard to tear apart.

So we are a long way forward from where we started, at Dr. Roger Wescott's timely observation that more and more "evidence has been accumulating of pre-Columbian transoceanic contact between the supposedly isolated hemispheres."

The ferocity of the attacks on Dr. Fell during the five months following the publication of his Pacific findings is mirrored in the wry reference to himself as a "crackpot Harvard professor." But Fell has all the attributes of a Frederic Wood Jones: superb scholarship stemming from ten years of specialized research and training at Harvard, preceded by study and fieldwork in New Zealand and elsewhere; exhaustive energies and indomitable tenacity in his search for the truth.

---

* So described in a classic letter to the *Saturday Review* (November 11, 1976) from Fell's Cambridge, Massachusetts-based colleague Professor C. Lamberg-Karlovsky of the American School of Prehistoric Research. Incensed by a "deeply disturbing" preview of *America B.C.*, the writer accused Fell of "nineteenth-century racism" for seeking to establish Old World roots in America, but offers no scientific rebuttal to his research.

14

During the half a millennium since Christopher Columbus made his intrepid, world-shaking voyage to the West Indies—a magnificent accomplishment that is in no sense diminished by the possibility that others may have preceded him—well over five hundred artifacts and/or similarities connecting the ancient Mediterranean to the Americas have been amassed by dedicated scientists.

This evidence indicates extensive pre-Columbian communication with the Americas across both the Pacific and south Atlantic oceans, as well as via the Icelandic/Greenland/Labrador route and along the accepted ten-thousand-year-old trans-Siberian/Alaskan trail.

The list of artifacts includes pyramids, obelisks, steles (inscribed upright stones that evolved into present-day gravestones), ball courts, colonnades, megaliths, musical instruments (trumpets, flutes, the Pan-pipe or syrinx, drums, tambourines), measuring scales, altars, crowns, tiaras, turbans, cosmetics, plumed headdresses, fans, thrones, litters, heraldic devices, sceptres, battle and ceremonial standards, drainage and air-conditioning systems identical in details, cups, plates, forks, spoons, pottery (identical pieces thousands of years old found in Ecuador and Japan), resin for incense, umbrellas (the friezes at Chacmultun portray two types still used in India and southeast Asia), papyrus reed and balsa boats, weapons, tools and ornaments made of obsidian (the volcanic glass well named the "steel of the Stone Age," used nine thousand years ago in the Mediterranean, in the South Pacific, in the Americas), amber, jade, ivory, basalt, greenstone (greenstone was being quarried on Mediterranean islands thousands of years before Christ), the boomerang (depicted in early Egyptian art and still used in Australia and southern India and by certain Indian tribes in Arizona and California), the chark (an early friction-induced fire-making device), and stucco (not a natural material but a combination of two "invented" products). Other Mediterranean–American connections include the sweet potato, maize, and banana (which had the same name on both sides of the pre-Columbian Atlantic); practices such as mummification, trepanning, and the blessing of water; similar myths (the Flood, the Tower of Babel, Adam and Eve, the serpent and the tree); a similar understanding of astronomy; and corresponding languages. The list could be extended to several pages, and a more complete rundown can be obtained from the New World Foundation in Orinda, California.

Opposite each of these items the Darwinians have remorselessly written down "coincidence."

Four not overly dramatic but immensely significant facts warrant special mention:

Spirulina. In the August, 1971, issue of *Ceres,* the magazine of the Food and Agricultural Organization of the United Nations, Geneviève Clement, a scientist of the French Petroleum Institute in Paris, reports under the title, "The Rediscovery of Spirulina," that a "forgotten species of protein-packed alga, eaten since time immemorial by the inhabitants of the Lake Chad area and, in Mexico, by the Aztecs, is now being commercially processed into an excellent infant food for future marketing in developing countries." (Possible connections between Lake Chad in Africa and the early Central Americas also were spotlighted when Thor Heyerdahl's epic-voyaging *Ra* was constructed by papyrus reed boat-builders from Lake Chad. The Norwegian explorer-scientist theorizes such boats in the New World were sailed and/or transported across the Atlantic from Africa.)

Cotton. The native American cotton that grows wild contains twenty-six small chromosomes. There is no indigenous variety with large chromosomes. European cotton, on the other hand, always contains twenty-six large chromosomes, with no small ones. Yet the cotton being cultivated by the American Indians when the Spaniards arrived contained twenty-six large and twenty-six small chromosomes. No one has ever provided a satisfactory explanation for this except that someone must have brought European cotton to America before Columbus and crossed it with the wild native cotton. There would have had to have been one parent with twenty-six large chromosomes and one with twenty-six small chromosomes.

Weaving. Since the beginning of history the peoples of the Mediterranean region have practiced two methods of weaving, *ikat* and *batik.* Both are highly complicated and sophisticated. In the ikat method, which is also practiced by the peoples of south and east Asia, parts of the warp or the woof are wrapped with waxed thread, or leaves, especially from palm trees, before the weaving begins. This keeps those parts free of color when the dyeing takes place. When the processed material is woven the designs take shape. In the batik method the cotton is first woven and the design is then covered with melted wax. During dyeing only the exposed portions are colored. The wax is then dissolved in boiling water or scratched off and the desired pattern emerges. The pre-Columbian American Indians practiced both methods, which puts a double strain on the coincidental factor.

Metallurgy. In "Man's first encounters with Metallurgy" *(Science,* 1964) Theodore Wertime, the celebrated authority on this subject, wrote:

> One must doubt that the tangled web of discovery, com-
> prehending the art of reducing oxide and the sulfide ores, the
> recognition of silver, lead, iron, tin and possibly arsenic and
> antimony as distinctive new metallic substances, and the
> technique of alloying tin with bronze, could have been spun
> twice in human history.

And yet the evolutionists would have us believe that two such tangled webs were spun in isolation from one another several thousand years before Columbus on both sides of the Atlantic.

Of all aspects of life in the New World, the one that impressed the Conquistadores the most was the exquisite workmanship and intricate technical skills shown in the production of ornaments of gold, silver, copper, bronze, and a number of alloys. And we now know that in South America the origins of this craftsmanship can be traced back for two thousand years before the Christian era (copper mining started about this date in Peru).

> Apart from their worth alone, the valuables were so fantastic
> in their novelty and originality that they seemed priceless. Nor
> is it likely that any of the princes known to us on earth
> possesses things of such or near such value.

So wrote Hernando Cortés to the Emperor Charles V. Most of these matchless treasures were speedily melted into shapeless lumps by the Spaniards. What has survived, including the great collection in the

New York Museum of Natural History, was mainly found in later excavations. Pierre Honoré (the pseudonym of an internationally known French scientist), author of *In Quest of the White God,* says of the New York collection: "The gold and silver plating is so extraordinarily fine and even, and sometimes so very thin, that it is hard to see how it could have been produced without a process akin to electrolysis."

One specific process described by Honoré should suffice to show how closely workmanship in the ancient Mediterranean paralleled workmanship in pre-Columbian America:

> The Manabis, on the coast of northern Ecuador ... made gossamer gold objects consisting of little grains, no bigger than half a pinhead, joined into ornaments. You have to look at them through a magnifying glass to appreciate the craftsmanship. They are magnificently worked, often soldered together from barely visible small parts, sometimes hollowed out and pierced as well. The Manabis must evidently have known and practiced the highly complex technique of "granulation," which was current in our own ancient civilizations. A little gold lion, only five-eighths of an inch high, was discovered at Knossos (Crete). It is made of two hollows soldered together, and its mane consists of many tiny gold balls of exactly equal size, fixed to their base. A gold duck, about one and a quarter inches high, also from Crete, shows this granulation at the wings and tail feathers. From ancient Pylos [modern Navarino in SW Greece] there is a toad one inch high, its warts of granulated gold, and an owl with wings indicated by means of these tiny gold balls. We know of similar gold objects from Troy, such as granulated gold purses and ear-rings, and also from the Etruscans.
>
> Probably the Sumerians originated this very special way of working gold. It is not only a question of fixing the little gold balls to their base, though making these balls is an art in itself. If they were soldered side by side on to a gold plate, they would quickly melt in the heat, flatten out and lose their ball shape. But if they are first heated in coal dust, their outer layers absorb carbon, melt more easily—and will do so at a temperature lower than the melting point of pure gold. If the balls are now put on to their base side by side, they will stick to it and one another at a low heat—too low to alter their shape—just because their surface melts so easily.

The technique is so ingenious that the scholars are convinced it cannot have been invented in two places.

Would anyone seriously consider eliminating such "artifacts" from a comparative study of ancient civilizations? For a more detailed examination of the subject see P. Bergsoe's works listed in the Bibliography.

Gold death masks, similar to those found at Mycenae and elsewhere—one of which inspired Heinrich Schliemann to send his famous telegram to the King of Greece: "I have gazed upon the face of Agamemnon"—have been discovered in the tombs of American Indians. Damascened ornaments (metal inlaid with gold and silver)—a process ascribed to Damascus—gorgon heads similar to those excavated at Syracuse, dogheaded gods, copper rivets for building, ceremonial axes, mosaics, sarcophagi, and head-shaped jugs provide additional prehistoric transatlantic links.

The oft-quoted summation by Dr. Stuart Piggott of Mycenaean/ British resemblances seems equally applicable to Mediterranean/pre-Columbian American similarities:

> Such resemblances may be individually fortuitous, but in their cumulative effect are too remarkable to dismiss.

In this category are the Mayans and Aztecs, and the Incas and pre-Incas. So much has been written about their superb astronomical accomplishments that only two sets of figures should suffice to position them on a par with ancient Egyptian, Sumerian, and Babylonian sophistication:

Length of Year
Actual sidereal	365.242,198
Gregorian calendar	365.242,400
Ancient Mayan	365.242,129

The early Central American figure is more accurate than our present calendrical one.

Length of Lunar Month
Actual	29.53059
Copan Mayan	29.53020
Palenque Mayan	29.53086

The correct figure falls between the two Mayan calculations. The Gregorian calendar is a makeshift of seven thirty-one-day months, four thirty-day months, and one twenty-eight-day month, which becomes twenty-nine every fourth year.

In his book *The Pacific Islanders* Professor Howells describes the proper method for establishing a hypothesis:

> Science, by contrast, projects a hypothesis from the facts at hand, and then looks for evidence which would disprove it. If the evidence is forthcoming the hypothesis is modified or discarded, a very painful thing to do as everybody knows.

Does this highly commendable process bear the slightest resemblance to the Darwinians' brushing aside every fact and artifact that doesn't support their views, while magnifying every shred of evidence that shores up their "familiar and so generally admired" edifice?

In addition to Dr. Wescott's observations of pre-Columbian transoceanic contact, he reveals two other "subversions": preglacial cartography and ancient aircraft.

No scientist has ever claimed that the two widely publicized Piri Reis maps in the National Museum of Turkey were forgeries.* Nor has anyone denied that they show preglacial details completely unknown in the sixteenth century.

American cartographer Arlington Mallerey, who researched these maps for many months with the U.S. Hydrographic Society, stated, in reference to Antarctica: "We don't know how they could have mapped it so accurately without an aeroplane."

"Preglacial cartography?" "Ancient aircraft?" To the barricades, gentlemen!

Four less well-known early maps offer comparable chronological problems. The pre-Columbian map of Zeno, dated 1380, shows Greenland without its present ice sheet. Investigations conducted by the French polar expedition headed by Paul-Emile Victor in 1947–48 confirmed mountain and river locations charted on this map.

---

* These maps came to light in 1929 at the old Imperial Palace, Istanbul. See Cyrus Gordon's *Before Columbus* (New York: Crown, 1971) for illustrations and background data: "There are features of the [principal] map which must antedate Columbus' discovery of America in 1492: notably, the essentially correct east coastline of South America in its right longitudinal relationship with the Atlantic coast of the Old World."

The 1513 map of Orontus Finaeus shows the Antarctica coastline with rivers and mountain ranges, which have been long buried under an ice cap. These locations were confirmed through ice soundings during the Geophysical Year of 1958.

The Flemish mapmaker Gerhardus Mercator (Gerhard Kremer)—who coined the word *atlas*—in 1538 published his first map of South America, prior to any significant exploration of that continent's west coast. It is considerably more accurate than one he published in 1569 after extensive exploration had been made; the 1538 map must have been based on unknown earlier sources.

Another map of Antarctica, published at Paris in 1737 by Phillipe Buache, shows the southern polar continent divided into two separate land masses. Not until 221 years later, again during the Geophysical Year of 1958, was this division confirmed through ice soundings.

The question of "ancient aircraft" leads naturally to the widely publicized, frequently photographed vast complex of straight lines, geometric patterns, and large-scale depictions of condors, spiders, and lizards etched out over several miles in the desert near Nazca, Peru. Visible only from the air, they are believed by a number of scientists to have served as a prehistoric astronomical atlas; the markings have yet to be satisfactorily explained, and make little sense in a strictly earth-bound context. Others, in North America, have attracted less attention.

At Brush Creek, Ohio, there is a huge serpent 1,348 feet long. At Poverty Point, where the Arkansas River enters the Mississippi Valley, is the oldest known geometrical site, which consists of six precisely laid-out octagons, one inside the other, with the outer figure measuring three-quarters of a mile across; its true nature was only discovered during an aerial survey in 1953, and radiocarbon testing has dated it to about 800 B.C.

Across the mid-continent of North America stretch a vast number of such constructions, which in most cases can be observed only from the air. Gerald Hawkins and other scientists are convinced that a high percentage of these served astronomical purposes.

At a 1976 international conference on prehistory in San Diego, California, sponsored by the Ancient Mediterranean Research Foundation, Dr. Egerton Sykes, Fellow of the Royal Asiatic Society and the "grand old man" of British antiquarians, declared that more would be learned about man's prehistory in North America than anywhere else in the world.

At the same conference I presented twenty-one original maps charting early migrations of *Homo sapiens,* which one professor of linguistics has termed a "new study of phonetic fossils." These represent about ten percent of over two hundred such maps charted during the past three years, and they are included here as additional supporting diffusionist evidence.

In my earlier book, *The Key* (1969), it was proposed that long before the Carthaginians and the Phoenicians—in some instances predating the Minoans—certain place-name elements traveled from the eastern Mediterranean all across the face of this planet (doing so primarily but not exclusively by sea). I suggested further that these elements, blended in an intricate, highly sophisticated fashion within "prehistoric" place-names (i.e., names that were there when the first historic travelers arrived on the scene and recorded them), could still be detected in widely separated parts of the world.

The charting of these above-mentioned maps has strengthened the belief that there were two migratory waves, the first truly global, the second widespread, often more intensive than the first, but conspicuously absent in some large regions.

Three primary place-name elements dominate the prehistoric scene:

1. *Hawwah* and its phonetic variants: *Hawa, Awa, Ava, Ua, Hua, Oa.* The Semitic name or word for the "Mother of all living"—Hawwah/Avvah, hence Eve, the first woman—appears to be the most logical origin point for this element.

2. *Eloah,* the Semitic name or word for "God," hence the Arabic Allah. An "Eloah" spelling has been recorded in a number of place-names: Aloa, Alua, Eloi, etc.; in others it has been recorded as Alawa, Alava, and so on, all such forms being phonetically identical.

3. *Oc/Og,* the earliest male fertility deity. Oc/Og permeated the mythology and religious cults of the ancient Mediterranean and was apparently disseminated to other parts of the world.

The three elements form six combinations:

Ala/Awa	Ala/Oc
Awa/Ala	Awa/Oc
Oc/Awa	Oc/Ala

On eleven of the twenty-one maps, place-names have been plotted that feature as their first two elements four of these combinations, one shown on a worldwide basis (in order to concentrate on the interhemispheric picture, the European region is not included; references to that portion of the world are, however, in the accompanying text). The two combinations omitted are in every respect as significant as the four shown.

In a number of instances all three elements are blended within the same place-name, usually as the sole elements. This occurs with such frequency that the suspicion grows that in pre-Christian times there existed a "trinity" composed of God, Woman, and Man—a more natural and less abstract concept than the present one.

Except for one sharply defined land trek across central Africa between the Near East and the Atlantic (a fertile, pastoral region five thousand to seven thousand years ago), the place-names appear exclusively in coastal and/or insular locations throughout the world. Such a pattern would appear to rule out the coincidental factor.

It is often argued that with human beings everywhere making the same sounds, one is bound to find phonetically similar place-names everywhere. If so, these names should be shotgunned all across the earth, being found literally everywhere.

This is not the case. The place-names under discussion are concentrated within narrow maritime ribbons encircling the globe, comprising only approximately two to three percent of present land areas.

On the ten additional maps are plotted place-names that feature four different initial elements. Although these names are also found in essentially maritime locations, the geographic patterns vary not only from the first group, with important regions excluded, but from one another. Such variations put an immeasurably greater strain on the coincidental factor because if their usage had sprung up through coincidence, these place-names too should be found everywhere.

The surface of this project has still only been scratched, but even the limited number of maps shown here indicate geographic routes that existed long before current linguistic and racial patterns emerged. Each of the twenty-one maps in itself offers factual evidence that runs counter to the accepted version of prehistory and early history. Again, at times one feels that two different planets are under examination.

The *Times Index-Gazetteer of the World* has been the primary source in the charting of these maps, providing the best available global data in terms of latitudes and longitudes. Occasionally, place-names have been secured from other standard reference works. Sufficient research has been conducted to establish that the more one probes in depth, the firmer the geographic patterns become.

Underlined vowels are assumed "lost"; the dropping of vowels is a process that has occurred time and again during the historic period, and which still continues. The *Times Index-Gazetteer* contains many place-names where there are current alternate spellings with and without vowels. (Otahiti one hundred years ago today is Tahiti. Wabash was first recorded as Awabasha, and so on.)

On maps 1–4 are plotted all of the *Awa + Ala* place-names listed in the *Times Gazetteer,* ranging from southern Arabia and the coast of Africa eastward to the Malay Peninsula, Indonesia, and Australia, then across the South Pacific to the west coast of South America, northward through Hawaii to the Washington/Oregon/Vancouver area, and on to Alaska.

It is hoped that all of the maps speak for themselves but some explanatory material accompanies them.

Space unfortunately rules out the inclusion of groups that appear to stem from three of the oldest known Near East place-names—districts of Mana and Tema, and the Kingdom of Saba or Sheba in southern Arabia, thought by some scholars to have been situated on both sides of the Red Sea. Each poses questions challenging the orthodox concept of our ancient past, as knotty as those raised by the maps shown here.

Overleaf: Maps 1–21 chart early migrations of *Homo sapiens.*

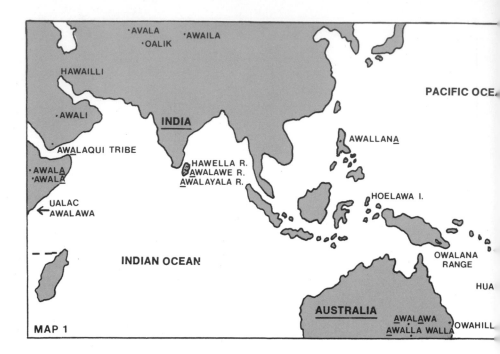

Maps 1-4: The combination of *Awa* + *Ala* + *Awa* predominates in maps 1-4: Awalawa, Hoelawa Island, Awalawa, Awalawa Heights, etc. Walla Walla (Washington and Australia) is proposed as *Awa* + *Ala* + *Awa* + *Ala*. Note two tight "trinities" on map 1, Ualac and Oalik, and two equally tight in Alaska (map 4), Lake Ualik and the Avalik River.

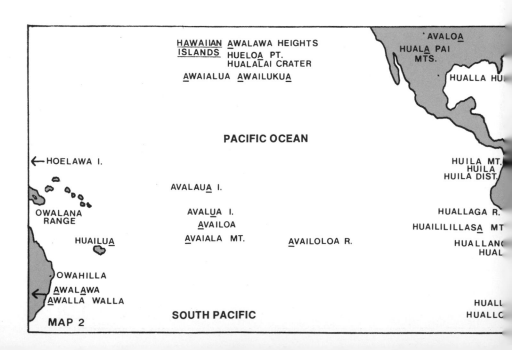

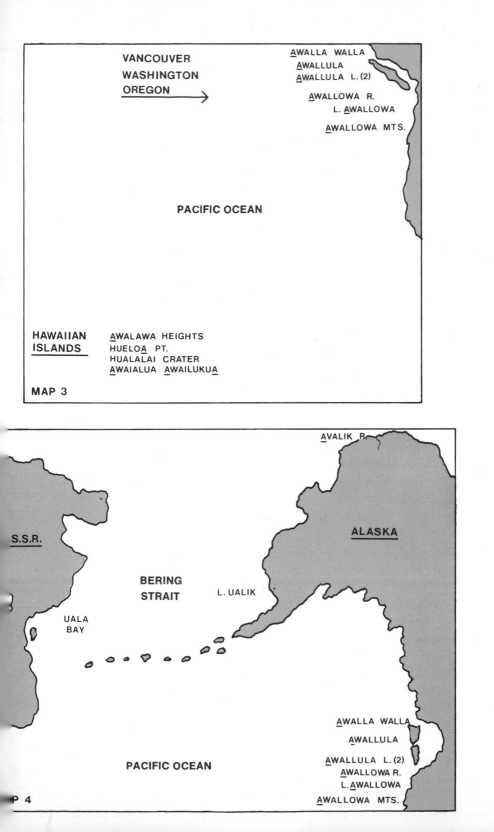

VANCOUVER
WASHINGTON
OREGON →

AWALLA WALLA
AWALLULA
AWALLULA L. (2)

AWALLOWA R.
L. AWALLOWA

AWALLOWA MTS.

PACIFIC OCEAN

HAWAIIAN
ISLANDS

AWALAWA HEIGHTS
HUELOA PT.
HUALALAI CRATER
AWAIALUA AWAILUKUA

MAP 3

AVALIK R.

S.S.R.

ALASKA

BERING
STRAIT

L. UALIK

UALA
BAY

AWALLA WALLA

AWALLULA

AWALLULA L. (2)

AWALLOWA R.

L. AWALLOWA

PACIFIC OCEAN

AWALLOWA MTS.

124

Maps 5-7: The two initial elements are reversed from maps 1-4. Both Halawa and Aloa place-names dot the entire route. Cape Alévéque, Australia (map 6), is a three-way blending, while Aluakaluak (map 5) repeats the proposed "trinity."

Map 7 follows Professor Fell's proposed route. See the *Boston Globe*'s map earlier in the text.

The same place-names appear in profusion along the coasts of Europe (not shown on the maps included here): *Scandinavia, Gulf of Bothnia:* Alevala, Oliwa, Olawa, Ullava, Ilawa, Ulava Sound, Hilloa, Alluaiva, Aloa, Holoa, Ello-ala, Halloala (2); *British Isles and adjacent continental coast:* Alawe River, Helouwa, Alawa River, Allowa, Ilawa, Ulava Islands, Alloa and Alloa Bay (Scot.), Lake Allua and Allua River (Ireland), Alloué, Aloue, Alouannec (France); *Spain:* Alava and river, Alloa, Olloa.

Such Scandinavian three-way blendings as Alavik, Alavik, Hollavik, Hillevik, are matched by the Allahuek Mountains and Alovech Province in the eastern Mediterranean.

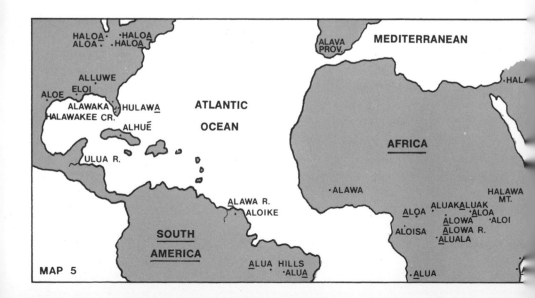

Top map:

CHINA

PACIFIC
OCEAN

•ALAWA
•ALAWARI

•ALAWA
•ALOI (7)

INDIA

HALLOWESA

ALUATOMA IS.
ALUATOMA MT.

LIWELI I.
HULUWA I.
AWALYA I.

ALAWATURA R.
HOLUWAGOA R.
HALAWATURE
HELAWA R.
ELLAWALA R.
ALAHEWA

ALOA
ALUA IS.

ALAWASA

ALAWEANA I.

ALUAKULUA

ALOA

ALAWA
MT.

ALAWELE
I.

C. ALÉVÉQUE

ALAWIK
REEF

• ULAWA I.

ALUAMOTUA R.

HOLOA

INDIAN
OCEAN

AUSTRALIA

L. ILLAWARRA

ILLAWARRA
ILLAWARRA

P 6

Bottom map:

HAWAIIAN

ISLANDS

WASHINGTON / OREGON ENCLAVE
ELLOA ALOE ALOA L.ELOIKA
ILAWACOA CAPE ALAVA

ALOALOA
HALAWA ALUALAILUA
OLOWALUA HALAWA
HALAWA ALEHAWA DIST.
ALOA V. HALAWA STREAM
HALEIWA

ALAEOAMALAVA

ALUATOMA IS.
ALUATOMA MT.

SOUTH

AMERICA

ALOA
ALUA IS.

PACIFIC
OCEAN

ULAWA I.
HOLOA

ALALOAMANUA

ALUAMOTUA R.

ALOAFAOA

ALEVUKA

L.ALALOANEA

ALALOA ALOA HOKOA ATOLL

ALOA R.

ALUAHIAPUA I.

ALUATAFITOA I.

L. ALLANACAN ELOA
ALAUATAROA &
SALT
ALAOA I. ELOISA MARSH
BAY
ULLOA PEN.

ILLAWARRA

ILLAWARRA (2)

ALEVERA I.

SOUTH PACIFIC

ALAUATAROA PK.

MAP 7

Maps 8-10: As a complete change of pace here are three maps featuring place-names in which the first two consonants are S followed by R. Map 8 shows these names proceeding via Jan Mayen Island along the coast of Greenland into North America. (No S/R place-names are listed for Iceland in the *Times Index-Gazetteer.*)

This chain of place-names terminates abruptly at Saranac Lake and Springs, and Saratoga and the Saratoga River, all upper New York State. (Saranac, Michigan, is apparently a historic transfer.) There are no other S/R place-names in North America westward to the Alaskan coast.

Map 9 follows S/R place-names across central Africa, up the north coast of South America, again terminating abruptly at Sarasota, Florida. One of the most inexplicable groups of place-names uncovered consists of Surinam and Sirinhaem, both coastal South America; Serinam, Madagascar; Surinam in an insular location east of Madagascar; and Surran-am (3) in southern Arabia. These are the only S/R/N/M place-names listed for this huge portion of the earth's surface and once more the coincidental factor is strained beyond credibility.

Map 10 charts S/R names through Siberia, ending with Sarana Bay, Alaska. No explanation offers itself for this three-way fringe intrusion of the North American continent except that in pre-Columbian times some group of people brought these names with them just so far and no farther. (The fact that Saranac, Saratoga, and Sarasota are three of the most famous watering places, or spas, in the New World evokes memories of Ponce de Leon's "Fountain of Youth.")

In what seems like another extraordinary "coincidence," the last S/R place-names westward in South America are Serrachoa Peak and Mountain on the Chilean coast (map 9), and some five thousand miles away across the South

Pacific, the last in a chain (not shown in our maps) of S/R place-names extending eastward from southern Arabia, is Serrukoa Island near Samoa: Serrachoa and Serrukoa, with nothing in between. (In these names, as well as many others, the three primary elements play major supporting roles, achoa/ukoa, etc.)

Maps 11-12: All place-names which begin with the *Oc/Og* + *Ala* combination listed in the *Times Index-Gazetteer* for the interhemispheric regions covered are charted on maps 11 and 12. It seems reasonable to say that these place-names could be transposed from one map to the other without materially altering the picture.

On Map 11 Okaloacoocche Swamp and Okalawaka are "trinity" blendings, as are Agalawa and the Agaleoa Islands on map 12. Ukalakua Island (map 12) combines Ok + Ala + Ok + Awa.

The word *ogallah,* used by a number of North American Indian tribes to describe their ancestral records and accomplishments, appears relevant in this context. With Og the only survivor of the Great Flood except for Noah and Co. in rabbinical mythology, the southeast Choctaw tribe's name for the "Survivor of the Great Flood"—Okalatabashih—is worth noting.

In other parts of the world the *Oc/Og* + *Ala* combination plays an equally prominent role. Note (not charted here) as additional blendings of the three

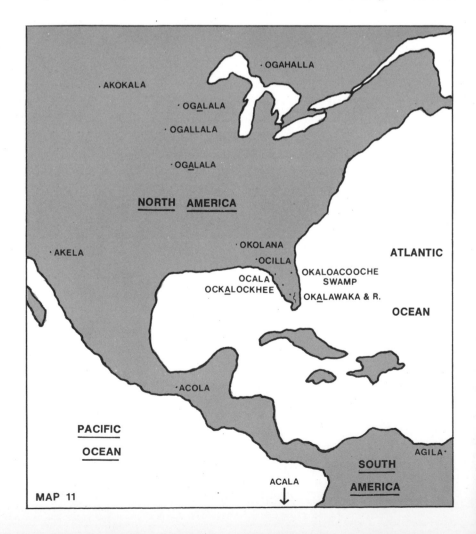

primary elements: Ukalahua Island in the Maldives; Agalawata and the Aggalawana River in Ceylon; islands that are a storehouse of key place-names, the Agulhué Islands in the South Pacific; Okulooa on the Southeast coast of Australia.

When one reverses the elements featured in maps 11 and 12 to the *Ala* + *Oc/Og* combination, some of the most thought-provoking of all the three-way blendings emerge: Alachua and Alaqua Creek, both in Florida; Halachoa; on the tip of the Mayan peninsula; the southeastern tribal names Alaguilac and Alikawa; Helechawa, Ohio; and of enormous stature, Allegawa, the first recorded spelling of Allegheny. In the same region such place-names as Alackawanna (a number of such locations), Alackawack, Alackawannock, Alackawaxen, names found in New York and Pennsylvania, appear to stem from the same source. These are Algonquin names found at forks in trails, and there are early spellings of Algonquin which suggest an Alagoanquin origin point.

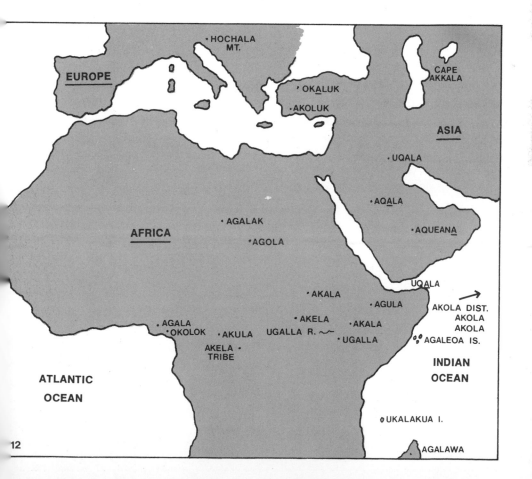

Maps 13 and 14: The *Oc/Og* + *Awa* place-names from the *Times Index-Gazetteer* charted on these two maps strengthen the suspicion that the classical word for "water"—*Aqua, Agua*—represents the tail end of a place-name combination of vast import in prehistoric times. (No satisfactory explanation of the second *Ua* element in Aqua/Agua has ever been put forward.)

Again place-names on both sides of the Atlantic are in many instances interchangeable. Certain names such as the two Capes Agua approaching the Strait of Gibraltar (map 14), Agua Island off the east coast of South America (map 13), and Aqua Volcano in Central America (map 13) may be historic "water" names, but it is impossible to classify as such Okoa Bay, the Ocoa Mountains, the Acua River in the Americas (all map 13), and Agoua, Ocua, Aquacocoa, Oguua, Aquanna, etc., in Africa (all map 14).

In a few instances there are Indian "water" meanings (map 13). Ocqueoc = "sacred water" (Algonquin). Quequeteant (not shown), the Indian name for Fall River, means "place of the falling water," and its proximity to Aquethneck (Rhode Island) suggests it was once Aquequeteant.

All three primary elements are enshrined in a number of New and Old World place-names. The origin of Aquilla, found in Alabama, Texas, and Ohio (map 13), is shrouded in mystery. Names of individual men and a relationship to the Latin *aquila* "eagle" have been proposed, but in their own areas the names are said to be of Indian origin. They match up with identical names on map 14 and the possibility appears likely that the royal bird, the

MAP 13

eagle, received its name from the three elements under discussion.
Ugueloa, the Mexican state of Ocoahila, Ockawalkee Creek, Akoeloekahuasa
(map 13), and Okawala, Ukawala, Aguellala, Aghouavila, and the Akoaluk
Mountains (map 14) are among other triple blendings.

For the last time, when the elements are reversed to *Awa* + *Oc/Og* (a
combination not shown on these maps), the overall picture is once more
greatly strengthened and brings the last of the six combinations into the text.
Oakalla (Texas), Awauchula (Florida), Huachacalla (coastal Chile) are
matched by Uacalla and Howakala Island, both coastal East Africa, and all
these names are part of a chain that is broken only by the Atlantic Ocean.

If just those place-names that are proposed as "trinities" could be charted on
one world map—which lies beyond the physical scope of this book—they
would form an extremely provocative pattern; when the pattern is supported
by those names featuring two of the three elements, there is nothing to
compare remotely with it in either prehistoric *or* historic times—except for the
"Saint" place-names, which we know were taken by European voyagers all
over the world during the past five hundred years. (Perhaps a thousand years
or more from now scholars will examine *those* St./San names and label them
"coincidences"!)

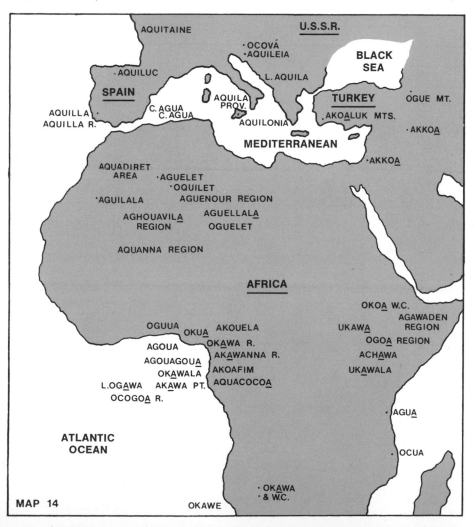

MAP 14

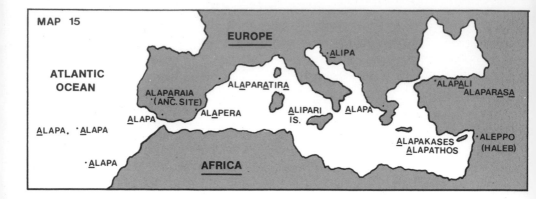

MAP 15

ATLANTIC OCEAN

EUROPE

AFRICA

·ALIPA

ALAPARAIA ·(ANC. SITE)

ALAPARATIRA

·ALAPALI
ALAPARASA

ALAPERA

ALIPARI IS.

ALAPA·

ALAPA

ALAPA. ·ALAPA

·ALAPA

ALAPAKASES
ALAPATHOS

·ALEPPO
(HALEB)

Maps 15-17: As place-names were segregated into various classifications, a small group situated in highly strategic locations gradually emerged. These names featured as their first two consonants L followed by P.

It was only when the end of this study was in sight that the positioning suggested that the ancient city of Aleppo (maps 15 and 16), the earliest known trading center between East and West, might be the origin point for this group of names. (Since the dawn of history Aleppo has also been known as Haleb.)

Three important prehistoric archaeological sites are plotted on map 15 in addition to Aleppo itself: Alaparaia in southwest Spain; the Alipari Islands north of Sicily; and Cyprus, with Alapathos (a port on the north coast) and Alapakases (the most fertile region), two of the oldest place-names, generally ascribed to the Phoenicians.

The names pick up southward on map 16 with Haleb Island in the Red Sea, and continue along the same African land route to the Atlantic. As in the Mediterranean, lost vowels are assumed for some names, not others (Alépé, Alapa, Elipa.)

These two maps would not warrant inclusion if it were not for what happens across the Atlantic on map 17. Here a cluster of Alapa names turns up in Alabama and Florida with the Alapahoochie and Alapaha rivers, tributaries of the Alab River, from which the state of Alabama takes its name. We are thus faced with a *double* transatlantic prehistoric transfer, Aleppo/Alapa, Halab/Alab, which in the absence of similar names along the coast of South America suggests travel via the Azores.

It is difficult to conceive, as in the case of the S/R place-names (maps 8 and 9), how local Indians, in isolation, would dream up these Alapa names and then take them no farther westward. (They are said to be Seminole names, while Alapocasa on the Delaware coast (map 17) is said to be Algonquin—meanings in all cases uncertain.)

There is another inexplicable mystery centered around this group of place-names in a far-off corner of the world not charted on these maps. Alapa names appear in coastal areas from southern Arabia to the east coast of Australia. Then, at the tip of North Island, one finds Alipera and Alipera Bay, the only place-names in all of New Zealand containing the letter L, which is not included in the Maori language.

No one knows how these twin names, identical in the first four syllables to Alaparasa, northeast of Aleppo, got where they are today, who brought them there, and when.

(None of the place-names charted on maps 1-14 are found in New Zealand.)

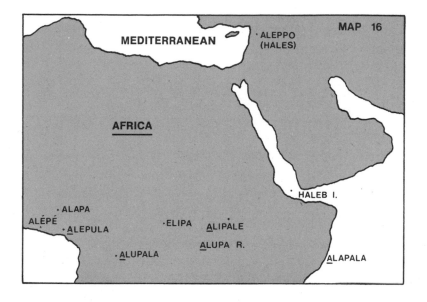

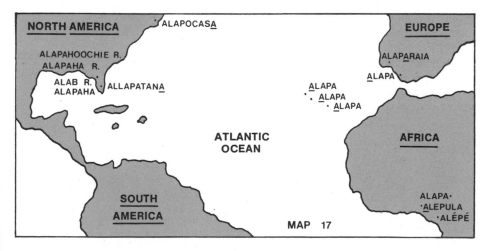

Maps 18-20: The T/R place-names charted on these three maps provided more excitement and surprises than any category included in the two hundred-odd maps. Three types of T/R names are plotted: plain Tara, Tara + Awa, and Tara + Oc/Og + Awa.

The T/R pattern differs from all others in that 1) the names do not follow the familiar land route across Africa but circumnavigate that continent, with a penetration into the East African area around Uganda (map 18); 2) although, like a number of secondary categories including S/R, they are not found in North America (map 18, top left; the Tara River is an Indian name but none appears beyond this), they are found in coastal and insular locations from the Middle East to Australia and also New Zealand (map 19), and do cross the South Pacific from New Zealand to the west coast of South America without appearing in Hawaii (map 20). It is the only category discovered that follows one route without following the other.

The same three forms of T/R place-names are found in profusion along the coastline of Europe from Turkey to Scandinavia, with a heavy concentration in Cornwall if one assumes a lost vowel in several hundred T/R names. Space has precluded the charting of these place-names.

In *The Key* it was suggested that the origin point for these names was Tareh, the father and brother of Abraham, but the pattern evolving on the maps suggests strongly the mysterious, prehistoric Tyrrhenians, who are known to have moved from Turkey at least as far as the west coast of Italy. There is little additional reliable data concerning them.

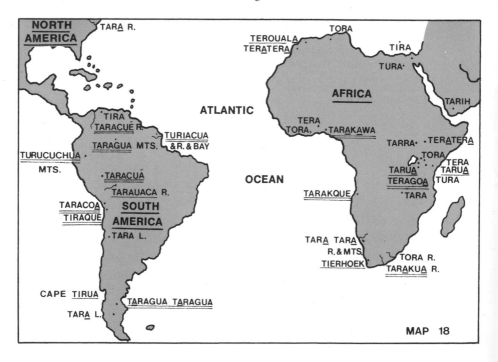

MAP 18

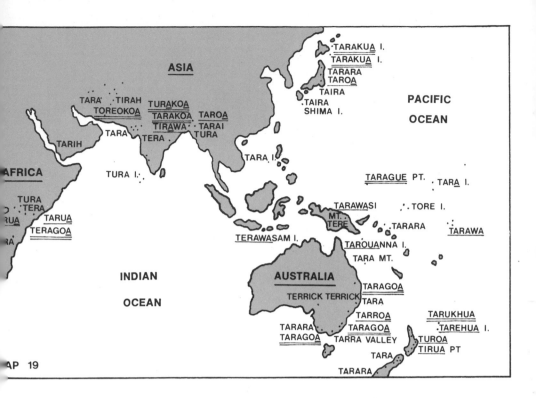

MAP 19

Map 19 labels:

ASIA

TARAKUA I.
TARAKUA I.
TARARA
TAROA
TAIRA
TAIRA
SHIMA I.

PACIFIC

OCEAN

TARA · TIRAH
TOREOKOA
TURAKOA
TARAKOA TAROA
TIRAWA · TARAI
TARA TERA TURA

TARIH

TARA I.

TARAGUE PT. · TARA I.

AFRICA

TURA I.

TARAWASI
MT.
TERE
TARARA
TARAWA

· TORE I.

TURA
TERA
TARUA
TERAGOA

RUA

RA

TERAWASAM I.

TAROUANNA I.
TARA MT.

INDIAN

OCEAN

AUSTRALIA
TERRICK TERRICK

TARAGOA
TARA

TARROA
TARAGOA
TARRA VALLEY

TARUKHUA
TAREHUA I.

TARARA
TARAGOA

TUROA
TIRUA PT

TARA

TARARA

TARA MT.

TARAGOA
TARA

TAROA
TARAGOA
TARRA VALLEY

TARA

TARARA

TARUKHUA
TUROA TAREHUA I.
TIRUA PT.

TERUA
· TERUA PEAK
· CAPE TIRUA
TERUA CHANNEL

TERUA

TARAKOI

TARAVAKA PK.
(EASTER I.)

SOUTH PACIFIC

TARACOA
TIRAQUE

CAPE TIRUA

TARAGUA TARAGUA
TARA L.

MAP 20

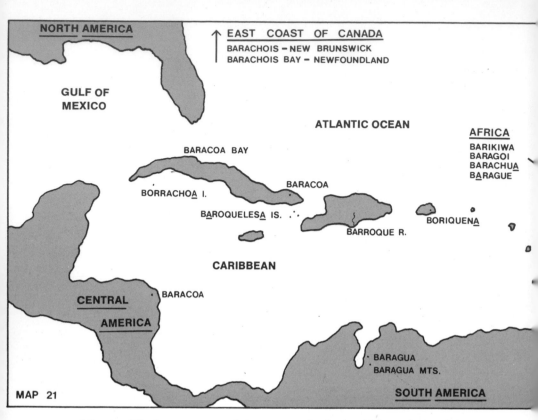

NORTH AMERICA

GULF OF MEXICO

ATLANTIC OCEAN

AFRICA
BARIKIWA
BARAGOI
BARACHUA
BARAGUE

BARACOA BAY

BORRACHOA I.

BAROQUELESA IS.

BARACOA

BARROQUE R.

BORIQUENA

CARIBBEAN

CENTRAL AMERICA

BARACOA

BARAGUA
BARAGUA MTS.

MAP 21

SOUTH AMERICA

Map 21: The largest group of place-names in the world is made up of those in which the first two consonants are B followed by R, and yet these names—densely concentrated in certain areas—are completely absent in huge portions of the earth: North America except for the east coast and one name in Alaska, Barra Bora, which bears a surprising resemblance to Bora Bora in the Society Islands, four thousand miles west of South America, the last name approaching from that direction. They are also not found in Hawaii and New Zealand. The pattern is essentially the same as the S/R place-names (maps 8-10), and certain other "second wave" categories, with one important exception—there are no B/R place-names between Iceland, where they abound, and the two Canadian coastal names Barachois and Barachois Bay.

The French spelling of these names is phonetically identical to the nine plotted on map 21 below, and to the four listed for Africa. It is impossible to rationalize how this *Bar + Oc/Og + Awa* combination arrived in New Brunswick and Newfoundland except by being taken there by pre-Columbian seafarers. The names could hardly have sprung up in isolation. About halfway along the three-thousand-mile coast between the West Indies and Canada is situated Burgaw, North Carolina, home of the Burgaw tribe, conceivably once Buragawa.

Most intriguingly, the last in a string of B/R place-names in Siberia, directly across the Bering Strait from Barra Bora, is Cape Barykova, a *Bar + Oc/Og + Awa* combination with a Russian accent.

Across the Atlantic the entire European coastline including the Mediterranean is lined with major seaports whose names begin with B/R: Bergen,

For different reasons Hawaii becomes of special importance in this study. First because of six words and/or names that are cloaked in ancient and profound significance, and second because of certain place-names that appear to have been transported from those islands into the Washington/Oregon/Vancouver enclave.

The six words or names are:

Hawaii itself, embodying *Hawa.* Links in a chain broken only by expanses of water extend from the *Awai* river on the eastern Mediterranean coast, a second *Awai* at the head of the Persian Gulf, the Huwayai river, Hawiyah, the Hawiyah salt marsh, and the Hawaya area, all in Arabia; and Avai and Hawaya on the adjacent African coast, eastward to Hawaii. Interspersed with these are a number of plain *Awa* place-names.

Hawaiki, a blending of the two primary elements *Awa* and *Oc/Og,* and an alternate form of Hawaii, found elsewhere in the Pacific, and phonetically identical to Havaiki, the traditional name for Raiatea in the Society Islands. Huachi is the most sacred of all names in Peru.

Ua, the Hawaiian word for "life," identical phonetically to *Hawwah,* the Semitic "Mother of all living."

Aloha, the Hawaiian greeting and farewell. When we examine the etymological ribbons flowing from the Mediterranean to both the British Isles and Hawaii, it seems likely that the earliest known form of the English greeting "hello"—*Alloa*—and *Aloha* might both stem from the Semitic name for "God," *Eloah.* At least it no longer merits the reaction of an English friend who when advised of this possibility several years ago peered over his spectacles and replied: "I say, that is a bit much."

Hula Hula, the ceremonial native dance. Another chain of place-names stretching from Hula, L. Hula, the Hula 'Emeq valley, Ula, and the Ulah tribe, all in the Near East, suggest that this name is a corruption of Ala Ala.

Ukulele, this traditional musical instrument, an accompaniment to the hula hula, is matched in spelling with a number of place-names that are proposed as part of the *Ok-ala-ala* category. The name is comparable to "small flea," but given its ritualistic status deserves a nobler origin.

Without research in depth, the following place-names found in Hawaii and the Washington/Oregon/Vancouver area have emerged.

Bremen, Brest, Bristol, Bournemouth, Biarritz, Bordeaux, Barcelona, Burgas, Beirut, to pull out a handful. Immense concentrations exist up the Ganges River and on the southeast coast of Australia, an extensive, unique pattern that again defies the laws of chance.

The North American mainland names appear in general unrelated to names found northward in Alaska or to the east:

Hawaii	*Washington/ Oregon/ Vancouver*
Akokoa Point	Ochocoa Mts., Creek, Res.
Okoi Bay	Hokoa River
Okawaihae	
Okahualui	
Aloa Volcano	Aloe
Aloaloa	Elloa
Alualailua	Aloa
Awalawa Heights	Awalla Walla
Hualalai Crater	Awallowa + R. + L.
Hueloa Point	Awallula + L. (2)
Halawa (4)	Cape Alava
Haleiwa	Ilawacoa
Olowalua	
Alehawa District	
Haleakala Crater	L. Eloika
Haleak Alakai Swamp	
Uwekuana	L. Owikenoa

Archaeological and related links between these two areas, separated by nearly two thousand miles of ocean, have been building up at an increasing pace.

Two overall aspects to this study of "phonetic fossils" merit final attention:

First, a preliminary probe in considerably greater depth, employing *Bartholomew's Gazetteer of the British Isles,* reveals that the various categories of place-names in England, Ireland, Scotland, and Wales also follow sharply defined geographical patterns that have apparently never been noted.

Running again directly counter to the coincidental factor, the place-names are *not* found everywhere. The only logical conclusion is that certain initial elements were of great significance to some prehistoric peoples in those islands but not to others.

All of the first three categories examined—the *Mana, Tara,* and *Awala* names—are predominantly in coastal and insular locations and all tie in with continental names, but of the three only the Awala group makes distinctive penetration along the Trent and Thames rivers into the heart of England.

The differences in positioning between the Mana and Tara groups are revealing, indicating that the names were brought into those islands by two separate seafaring pre-Celtic peoples. (The continental patterns bear no relationship to the known migrations of the Celts.)

The two T/R counties in Ireland—Tyrone and Tirconnell (today Donegal), both in the northwest—contain a high proportion of "Tara" names which follow Lough Erne eastward. The famous Tara is in County Meath and there are similar names elsewhere in the island.

The M/N place-names are found in large numbers in Limerick County and follow the Shannon River into the interior, then step up in Monaghan County and around the Main River in the northeast.

There are more T/R place-names per square mile in Cornwall than anywhere else in the world, including fifteen Tar + Awa and five Tar + Oc/Og + Awa names listed in Bartholomew's.

Interior English counties such as Surrey, Berkshire, Oxfordshire, Bedfordshire, Wiltshire, Northamptonshire, Warwickshire, and Leicestershire are either totally devoid of both T/R and M/N place-names or contain one or two each, yet the presence of both groups along the east coast from Scotland to Kent rules against these names having been obliterated in subsequent Anglo-Saxon invasions.

Enough spadework has been done on other groups to strengthen the belief that the bewildering series of prehistoric seafaring migrations described in Irish mythology—generally put down to medieval monkish interpolations—is based on fact.

Finally, the most mysterious worldwide aspect of this study is that in quite a startling number of instances place-names at the "end of a line" are double-barreled.

Bora Bora in the Society Islands and Barra Bora in Alaska are good examples. Also Walla Walla in Australia and Walla Walla in Washington, each the last in a series. Wagga Wagga is situated near Walla Walla in Australia.

Some T/R cases are especially provocative: Taragua Taragua on a river at the extreme tip of South America is at a dead end, as is Terrick Terrick in Australia. Teratera is the end of the line coming around the northwest coast of Africa, and except for Tarakque some distance to the north the Tara Tara Mountains and river occupy what might be considered a comparable location on the southwest coast.

Alacalac is the final link in an *Ala* + *Oc/Og* chain that terminates on the southeast coast of Australia. Crossing over from Africa to South America, one leaves behind a number of coastal *Ua* and *Oa* names to encounter as the first comparable name in Brazil the Uaua River, which to some ancient seafarer after a successful transatlantic journey may at the time have seemed like the end of the line.

Aloaloa and Akoakoa in the South Pacific are also strategically situated. The names above all turned up without a search being made for them. The only explanation that comes to mind is that early voyagers might have used a double-barreled signature to indicate to future travelers that they had come so far and no farther. At least no other rational possibility has suggested itself, and pure coincidence again strains credulity.

Mulling over the entire network of prehistoric place-names, I remember a comment made several years ago. A batch of large-scale forerunners of the maps exhibited here was being shown for the first time to Barry Winkleman of the *Times* (London), a down-to-earth, extremely well-informed atlas publisher I had never met before.

He had examined only five or six of them, which were spread out on his office floor, when he looked up, cocked his head, and asked: "Have you read Von Däniken's *Chariots of the Gods?*"

It was most impressive that this thoroughly mundane (in the literal sense) evidence sent someone else's thoughts soaring beyond the confines of our native planet.

15

*We shall move out there, not because we want to but because we have
to. . . . If we add to our present technology just one thing—thermonuclear
power—we shall have the capability of moving out to the stars and
colonizing them. . . . The whole history of evolution has been the
production of colonists and it seems doubtful that any planning, however
brilliant, could produce individuals as well suited to be colonists as we
have arrived at by the trial and error method of evolution.*

—DR. EDWARD S. GILFILLAN, JR., *Migration to the Stars*

With Darwin's theory gradually conquering the minds of humanity,
his disciples eventually found themselves in a position where they
could quite rightly ask: "If a Genesis-type creation did not take place,
how else could *Homo sapiens,* except through the evolutionary process,
have got here?"

The burden of proof was shifted onto the shoulders of those who,
discarding the biblical version of man's origin and yet refusing to
include him within the framework of terrestrial nature, failed to come
up with some logical third alternative to evolution or Genesis. Until
after World War II none seemed available.

If someone had suggested in 1858 that *Homo sapiens,* as a fully
evolved species, had arrived here from somewhere else in com-
paratively recent times to colonize this planet he would no doubt have
been quietly bundled off to the nearest nursing home. And until the
late 1940s such a proposal would have been generally regarded as the
hallucinations of a crackpot.

The situation has now changed so radically that we have not yet had
time to grasp its enormous implications. As one prominent London
scientist commented to me in the spring of 1976: "During the first

forty years of my life I wouldn't even have discussed the possibility of man's extraterrestrial evolution. But since human beings succeeded in landing on the moon, I think almost anything could have happened in our past. And anything may happen in our future."

It now appears certain that no other planet in our system is inhabited by rational beings (if by any form of life). And yet science is pressing on toward the infinite, convinced that at some point its quest will prove successful.

A dramatic boost to morale was provided on January 19, 1977, when it was announced from Munich that a joint team of German, American, and French astronomers using the German one-hundred-meter Effelsher radio telescope—the largest movable instrument of this type in the world—had discovered water in a galaxy 2.2 million light years from earth.

While the discovery brought forth jubilant reaction around the globe, there was little surprise in scientific circles. Expressing the general opinion that water vapor clouds will be found in other galaxies, Dr. Otto Hachenberg, director of the Bonn Institute for Radio Astronomy, stated he was confident that "somewhere conditions exist like those on earth which are conducive to development of living organisms."

Further clarifying the significance of the discovery, a spokesman for the Max Planck Institute in Munich added: "One can therefore expect to find planets revolving around a sun, having perhaps developed similar environmental conditions to those of the planets in our solar system."

More and more money, time, and energy are being poured each year into optical, radio, and X-ray astronomy, over and above the mammoth annual amounts spent by the American and USSR space programs, both motivated to some degree by the belief that life exists elsewhere in the universe.

Because of atmospheric conditions, the largest optical telescope on earth, the two-hundred-inch installation at Mount Palomar, California, can be used less than fifty nights a year and may prove to be the limit of terrestrial astronomy. A huge, multipurpose observatory orbiting in space is planned for the 1980s. Reflecting telescopes, special equipment for examining the sun, X-ray detectors, and a radio telescope will be installed.

This new space observatory will be free from atmospheric interference. To give some idea of its capabilities, the Mount Palomar telescope can survey moon craters three thousand feet in diameter, but the same size telescope in orbit will be able to detect those only three hundred feet across, a thousand percent improvement. Though the optical examination of the universe outside our system will be comparably stepped up, many scientists see the space observatory as only an intermediate stage before a land-based installation is constructed on the dark side of the moon.

The use of radio astronomy has increased to a staggering degree the distances that can be monitored, encompassing sound waves emanating from as far off as the Crab Nebula, twice as far from earth as Nebula "IC 133," where water has been discovered.

Cambridge astronomer Sir Fred Hoyle has compared our problems in trying to interpret possible radio signals to a frontiersman holed up in a log cabin without a telephone. Sound waves are zooming over him but he can't connect with them. Dr. Carl Sagan, a leading American astrophysicist, has likened our predicament to an island full of South Sea island aborigines. All sorts of sound waves from more advanced parts of the earth are passing right through them without the natives' being aware of it.

In November, 1976, the most ambitious project yet designed to try to detect radio signals between civilizations in the outer universe was announced. Labelled SETI (The Search for Extraterrestrial Intelligence), the project will involve a number of observatories, coordinated by the two NASA (National Aeronautics and Space Administration) laboratories in California—the Ames Research Center in Mountain View and the Jet Propulsion Laboratory at Pasadena, operated by the California Institute of Technology.

The initial objective is to construct an analyzer that can examine a star and its possible planets at the same time through one million radio-frequency "peepholes." The search will be concentrated on frequencies lying between 1420 megahertz (those emitted by hydrogen atoms) and 1662 megahertz (those emitted by hydroxyl atoms), the so-called "waterhole" of the radio spectrum.

NASA reasons that different galactic species might meet there just as terrestrial species have always met at certain more mundane "waterholes"—at the most logical place for us to pick up signals between other intelligent beings.

The following incident highlights the controversy that has raged for some years between those scientists who believe we should try to announce our presence to more advanced civilizations in hopes of receiving help from them, and those who are convinced we should lie low and let well enough alone. In the same month that SETI was announced, a round-the-earth storm erupted when it was reported in the *New York Times* (November 4) that "Sir Martin Ryle, Nobel laureate in physics and Britain's Astronomer Royal, is trying to persuade the world's radio astronomers to refrain from informing possible civilizations in space of the existence of intelligent life on this planet, lest the earth be invaded by hostile beings." Although Sir Martin did not deny that such an appeal had been addressed to the International Astronomical Union, he vigorously stated the next day that he was in no fear of invasion from outer space. And yet no other explanation for his making such an appeal was put forward.

Those who are puzzled or perturbed as to why such an enormous, costly, constantly expanding effort is being directed toward the exploration of the universe outside our solar system will find the detailed reasons set out for the first time by the eminent scientist Dr. Edward S. Gilfillan, Jr., in *Migration to the Stars* (1975). We are taken behind the scenes on a guided tour into an area which until now has been familiar only to topflight astronomers and scientists working in related fields. Updating the situation into what can only be described as a state of extreme urgency, he greatly clarifies a widely publicized statement made by Carl Sagan in the 1960s:

> I cannot say I believe there is life out there. All I can say is that there are a number of reasons to think it is possible and that we have at our command the means of finding out. These two things being the case, I would be very ashamed of my civilization if we did not try to find out.

Based in large part on lectures delivered at the Lowell Technological Institute and the Chinese University of Hong Kong, Gilfillan's landmark document drastically and irrevocably alters prevailing concepts of man's place in the universe, with special emphasis on the role outer space must play in our destiny if the human race is to survive.

Gilfillan not only delves deeply into all of the foreseeable problems involved in the conquest of outer space, but works out solutions to these problems, employing only proven technology and readily available materials (except for thermonuclear power, which is anticipated during the next several decades).

In his analysis of mankind's current situation on this planet, Dr.

Gilfillan is considerably less of a pessimist and gives us a bit more precious time than many of his fellow scholars. Reviewing the seven types of catastrophes that might overcome us—nuclear war, pollution, overpopulation, depletion of resources, inadvertence ("actions taken before we know enough about what we are doing"—those involving DDT, aerosols, drugs, food preservatives, and biological agents such as bacteria, viruses, enzymes, etc.), futility,* and the terminal laboratory experiment—he expresses the opinion that we could handle any one or possibly two of the first six, if we could devote our total attention to it or them. However, echoing the views written by Sir Charles Darwin in 1958, he believes we are simply not in a position to do this and will probably become increasingly less so.

The terminal laboratory experiment (action taken by a dedicated scientist who is well aware of the risk involved but goes ahead notwithstanding) is the one type of catastrophe he feels is "truly inevitable" and he cites several examples where we have knowingly taken such gambles in the past, notably the second atomic bomb dropped into the sea at Bikini. Yet even here he calculates we may well escape such a final disaster for another two centuries.

This is a generous reprieve compared to a number of other specialists, including Dr. Dennis L. Meadows of MIT (see *Chemical and Engineering News*, March 16, 1972), who are convinced that ultimate catastrophe will occur about the middle of the next century, roughly seventy years from now.

The immediate reaction of at least one reader to the data presented was one of gloom and depression at the seeming inevitability of our being forced to abandon a terrestrial way of life which, in spite of obvious hardships, has become sweet and deeply cherished. Nor is it comforting to think of the dislocations and potential disasters our children and their children may face.

And yet, as one absorbs the material and its true significance becomes apparent, a growing sense of elation replaces despondency. For Dr. Gilfillan makes clear that there is literally a way out, that radiant hope could lie beyond the foreboding horizon, hope that may well supplant current futility.

---

* Dr. Seymour B. Sarason, Professor of Psychology and Urban Education at Yale, in an article "Growing Up Old" *(Yale Alumni Magazine,* December, 1976), writes pertinently on the subject of futility: "The sense of aging has already begun in young people, and their sense of the passage of time has become related to the sense that time is a limited resource already beginning to run out."

Nearly a decade ago Dr. E. Leo Sprinkle, Professor of Psychology at Wyoming University, expressed the view that we may be approaching the "most exciting and challenging period in man's history." Gilfillan, his Massachusetts-based fellow scholar, supports this opinion with concrete, accepted facts. Given sufficient moral strength and unity of purpose, he believes that "this is the beginning of an age of discovery and expansion without end. There is so much to do out there that there can never again be enough people to do it."

Most pertinent to the main thesis of this book—i.e., that mankind may be caught up in a universal process of evolution that could not have been envisioned by Darwin, Huxley, and Haeckel on the basis of the facts available to them—is Dr. Gilfillan's conviction that terrestrial overpopulation, rather than being an insurmountable problem, is a requirement for the logical next step in *Homo sapiens'* evolution:

> It appears that the space about the earth could accommodate a population more than a hundred times as large as we have now, and we may need a population that big if we are to move out of the solar system and colonize the planets of the stars.

The possibility raised earlier here that the "original primary purpose of *Homo sapiens* was to populate this globe" becomes far more realistic within such a vastly expanded context.

As one reads through *Migration to the Stars,* which, no matter what our future holds, will remain as one of the first detailed analyses of what that future can be like, the thought constantly recurs: If it is possible for us, fledglings in space, to move *out* in such a manner, is it not probable that one of the far more technologically advanced outer space civilizations which Dr. Harlow Shapley and many others (including Dr. Gilfillan) believe exist has successfully moved *in* from the opposite direction? Colonizers from such a civilization could very well have been our direct ancestors.*

---

* Dr. Gilfillan states: "Judging from our experience here many planets should have developed technological cultures by now, and if we have a good chance of colonizing planets so had they. Some of them should have made it long before us, say a billion years earlier." He suggests that the rings of Saturn "may be the remains of a community of orbiting space stations. . . . No satisfactory theory which accounts for them has ever been advanced. It is known from radar observation that whatever these rings are made of it is there in fairly large chunks, a yard or more in maximum dimension." He continues: "As for fossils of colonists from space, we may already have them. The fragments of bones we now attribute to early man could just as well have come from space men." And supporting my own views, he inclines to the hypothesis that "the total number of feasible evolutionary paths from a chemical to an electromechanical culture is so restricted that any who achieve it must be very like ourselves."

16

The leapfrogging strategy proposed for our continuing ventures into space, and suggested as perhaps already having been employed by other more advanced technological cultures, brings into the limelight an obscure file of nearly five hundred case histories that has accumulated during the past three centuries.

These deal with certain inexplicable objects that have been observed in the vicinity of the sun, the moon, and the other planets in our solar system.

In the large majority of these incidents astronomers of the highest professional reputation were involved. At the time, some caused intense speculation among scientists. In the light of recent space developments they may warrant more attention than they are given.

Galileo, Kepler, and Copernicus all noted on occasion the passage of mysterious bodies through the heavens, but the most celebrated early sighting was made by a member of the Cassini family—originally Italian but naturalized in France during the reign of Louis XIV—five or six members subsequently making Cassini the most distinguished name in French astronomy.

Jean Dominique Cassini, born near Nice in 1625, had already established the times of the rotation of the planets Jupiter, Mars, and Venus and discovered four of the satellites of Saturn, when in the late night sky of January 25, 1672, he observed near Venus an unfamiliar luminous object. It was visible through his telescope for about ten minutes and Cassini wrote down the details of the sighting.

Fourteen years later, at 4:15 in the morning of August 18, 1686, he again observed what he believed was the same unknown satellite. It was visible for about fifteen minutes, appearing to be approximately one-quarter the size of the planet. All details were again recorded.

No satisfactory explanation of Cassini's two sightings was offered, although since his son was a member of the Royal Society of London and an intimate of Newton and Halley (a later descendant became Director of the Paris Observatory), they continued to be a subject of no small interest.

Venus was under continual surveillance during the years following Cassini's second sighting, but it was not until October 23, 1740, that the Scottish astronomer James Short—a Fellow of the Royal Society and designer and builder of the largest telescope constructed up to that time (commissioned by the king of Spain)—observed for over an hour what he described as an unknown "body" near Venus. Short estimated it to be approximately one-third the diameter of that planet. If it was the same object twice observed by Cassini, no acceptable explanation was ever given as to where it had been during the previous fifty-four years.

Another nineteen years followed Short's discovery and then on May 20, 1759, what appeared to be the same body was studied for over half an hour through the telescope of a German astronomer, Andreas Mayer of Griefswald. Two years later it was observed at different times of the year by four well-known astronomers, three in France and one in Denmark.

Joseph Louis Lagrange of Marseilles, who some time after became the director of the Berlin Academy of Sciences, reported seeing it on February 10, 11, and 12, 1761. The following month Jacques Montaigne of Limoges saw it on the third, fourth, seventh, and eleventh, and the astronomer Montbarron of Auxerre on the fifteenth, twenty-eighth, and twenty-ninth. In June, July, and August the Danish scientist Roedkioer found it on eight occasions in the lens of his telescope at Copenhagen.

Another lapse intervened until January 3, 1768, when Christian Horrebow also observed it at Copenhagen—after which it disappeared for 118 years.

As can be imagined, the erratic pattern of appearance, disappearance, and reappearance followed by total absence—with intervals of fourteen, fifty-four, nineteen, two, and seven years between sightings—divided the astronomical world into two camps: skeptics and believers. In the face of the combined reputations of the observers and their meticulous recording of events, the opposition was left with few arguments except to reiterate that "it couldn't have happened."

By 1886 the debate had become more or less academic when

suddenly it flared up all over again. In that year the French astronomer J. C. Houzeau de Lehaye reported observing what sounded suspiciously like the long-lost satellite. Since no one during the next six years confirmed his sightings, the argument might again have simmered down if it had not been for the identity of the next observer.

Edward Emerson Barnard in the 1890s enjoyed a worldwide scientific reputation second to none. The American astronomer had discovered a star in the constellation Ophiuchus which was named in his honor. Even more important he had discovered the fifth moon of the planet Jupiter.

It so happened that, like Dr. F. A. P. Barnard, president of Columbia University, Edward Emerson Barnard was an extremely eloquent and persuasive doubting Thomas, a leader of the group who branded Houzeau's findings, along with the earlier observations of the Venusian mystery, as "absurd" and "ridiculous." Scientifically, they could not be fitted into the accepted order of things.

Then, on August 13, 1892, Barnard himself literally saw the light. He reported, undoubtedly with some embarrassment, that he had observed an unknown object of "seventh magnitude" in the vicinity of Venus. Afterward it vanished and has never been seen again. It was as though it had staged its final appearance solely to convince Barnard of its existence.

The situation today is what it has been during the last 305 years, since Jean Dominique Cassini's initial sighting in 1672. No one really knows what the unidentified object was, where it came from, or where it went. There are, of course, no natural laws that can explain such a pattern.

An equally baffling mystery involving a huge object, or series of objects, observed in the vicinity of the sun attracted a great deal of attention from the scientific world and the general public during the mid-nineteenth century.

At that time Urbain Jean Joseph Leverrier was one of the world's most distinguished astronomers. Among other notable mathematical studies, Leverrier had calculated where a then unknown planet would be for some time after August 19, 1846. His figures were transmitted to Johann Gottfried Galle in Berlin, who received them on September 23. During the following night, the German astronomer located through his telescope a star of the eighth magnitude—exactly where Leverrier had predicted it would be. It was the planet subsequently called Neptune.

By 1859 Leverrier was commander of the French Legion of Honor and Director of the Paris Observatory, a post in which he had been preceded by one of the Cassinis. On March 26 of that year a relatively unknown astronomer, a Dr. Lescarbault of Orgeres, observed for an hour and a half an unfamiliar object moving across the face of the sun.

Lescarbault wrote to Leverrier telling him of his findings, and after a long interview at Orgeres, the Paris Observatory director, comparing the doctor's calculations with earlier sightings of a similar object near the sun (Fritsche, October 10, 1802; Stark, October 9, 1819; De Cuppis, October 30, 1839; and Sidebotham, November 12, 1849), announced that Lescarbault had discovered a new planet between Mercury and the sun. Leverrier estimated that its mass was one-seventeenth of Mercury's, with an orbit of nineteen days, and he bestowed upon it the name Vulcan.

The news naturally created a sensation, especially in France, where Napoleon III swiftly elevated Dr. Lescarbault to the Legion of Honor. Shortly after, Vulcan vanished.

Similar unknown objects, or possibly the same one, had been seen crossing the sun's disk on at least two previous occasions, neither of which was used by Leverrier in his calculations: On August 9, 1762, an astronomer from Basle, M. de Rostan, was in Lausanne taking altitudes of the sun when he was astonished to see through his telescope a strange, spindle-shaped body "approximately three of the sun's digits in breadth and nine in length," which was proceeding "at no more than half the velocity with which the ordinary solar spots move." He continued to follow its progress until September 7, when it reached the edge of the sun and disappeared.

During this twenty-nine-day period an object fitting de Rostan's description, except for a slight discrepancy in breadth, was observed by another astronomer, M. Croste, at Sole, about one hundred miles due north of Lausanne.

Commenting on the two separate but simultaneous series of observations, the editor of the *Annual Register* (London, 9:120) stated: "In a word, we know of nothing to have recourse to, in the heavens, by which to explain this phenomenon."

In the *Times* (London), January 10, 1860, the year after Leverrier's announcement of Lescarbault's planetary discovery, an article told how the astronomer Benjamin Scott, City Chamberlain of England's capital city, had observed what was apparently the same celestial traveler during the summer of 1847. Scott stated that he had seen through his telescope an object "approximately the size of the planet Venus" moving across the sun.

He had so doubted his own sense of sight that a public announcement was not made, but that same evening he had discussed it with a Fellow of the Royal Astronomical Society, Dr. Dick, who had "cited other instances." On January 12 a letter appeared in the *Times* from Richard Abbott, another Fellow of the R.A.S., who stated that Scott had written to him at the time of the occurrence explaining what he had seen.

Leverrier did not waver in his conviction that Lescarbault had located another planet. After lengthy calculations similar to those that had led to the discovery of Neptune, he predicted that Vulcan would be visible telescopically on March 22, 1877. Observation posts were set up at Madras, Melbourne, and Sydney, and in New Zealand, Chile, and the United States. M. Struve, grandfather of Otto Struve, was in command of the operation in Siberia and Japan. This encompassed the area in which Leverrier believed the lost wanderer would be visible.

(The week before the expected arrival, the editor of *Nature* wrote that it was difficult to explain how six observers, "unknown to one another," at widely separated times and places should have "data that could be formulated, if they were not related phenomena." On March 20, 1862, the astronomer Lummis had seen what Leverrier believed was the same object.)

The great day came and went but there was no sign of Vulcan. Nor has the mysterious visitor ever made a return appearance. Leverrier died a few months after what must have been the biggest disappointment in his life.

On July 29, 1878, the year following the nonappearance of Vulcan, during a total eclipse of the sun, visible in the Colorado/Wyoming area of the United States, two well-known American astronomers observed from separate points a *pair* of "shining objects at a considerable distance from the sun."

Professor James Watson of the University of Michigan picked them up through his telescope at Rawlins, Wyoming. Professor Lewis Swift, whose work on nebulae had won him international recognition, watched them through his telescope at Denver, Colorado, 123 miles south and 136 miles east of Rawlins.

The two scientists were immediately attacked by the skeptics, who, apparently unaware that the distance between them would affect their calculations, argued that the two sightings did not conform with one another. Others claimed that they had mistaken stars for unknown objects. Swift replied in *Nature* (September 19, 1878) that when the relative positions were taken into account, his observation "was in close approximation to that given by Professor Watson."

As for the objects being stars, Watson wrote in the *Observatory* (2:193) that he had "previously committed to memory all stars near the sun, down to the seventh magnitude," and that there was absolutely no question that the unfamiliar bodies were stars. Swift declared in *Nature* (21:301): "I have never made a more valid observation, nor one more free from doubt."

Those who would like to check further the reliability of the two astronomers are referred to the *American Journal of Science* (116:313), in which Professor Swift gave a meticulously detailed description of what he saw, and *Monthly Notices* (38:525), in which Professor Watson made an equally careful presentation of his facts.

Before discussing certain phenomena that have been observed in the vicinity of the moon, we should note that in 1894, 1903, and 1911 luminous unidentified objects were seen near the planet Mars. Several of these sightings were made at the Lowell Observatory by two famous U.S. astronomers, Percival Lowell and Edward Charles Pickering, the first a brother of Harvard University's eminent president, Abbott Lawrence Lowell, and the equally eminent poet Amy Lowell; the second from a family which subsequently produced two more distinguished astronomers.

Unidentified luminous objects crossing the face of the moon or in its vicinity on numerous occasions during the past few centuries have been reported by other top-ranking scientists, and such reports are continuing to come from equally qualified sources.

A number of these mysterious sightings were made in the late eighteenth century by Sir William Herschel, whose extraordinary contributions to astronomy included the discovery of Uranus and its satellite "children," the sixth and seventh satellites of Saturn, the spots at the poles of Mars, the rotation of Saturn's ring, the belts of Saturn, the rotation of Jupiter's satellites, and the daily periods of Saturn and Venus.

Herschel's professional standing was so unassailable that when on several occasions during the 1780s he announced the observation of inexplicable luminous bodies on or near the surface of the moon, no one dared challenge or ridicule him, at least not publicly. To Herschel there was no natural explanation for these lights.

Similar observations were made throughout the nineteenth century. One scientist told of seeing what "looked like a star crossing the moon," and then hastened to add, "which, on the next moment's consideration, I knew to be impossible." In *Science* (July 31, 1896) the director of the Smith Observatory, W. R. Brooks, gave details of a "dark, round object" which passed "rather slowly across the moon in a horizontal direction." About this time there was a flurry of comparable sightings.

On January 27, 1912, in *Popular Astronomy* (20:398) Dr. F. B. Harris reported that he had seen on the face of the moon "an intensely black object." He estimated its size to be "250 miles long and 50 miles wide." In a measured understatement Dr. Harris said of his experience: "I cannot but think that a very interesting and curious phenomenon happened."

In 1968 the American National Aeronautics and Space Administration (NASA) published a pamphlet entitled "Chronological Catalogue of Reported Lunar Events." The publication gives a long list of unexplained sightings of "both stationary and moving" lights in the immediate vicinity of the moon. Descriptions are also included of "perfectly circular craters (on the surface of the moon) that look more like domes and which in some cases are in perfect alignment, and glowing mists and sudden patches of gem-colored outpourings."

Two hundred years after Sir William Herschel's remarkable lunar observations, one finds Dr. Carl Sagan stating: "Intelligent beings from elsewhere in the universe may have—or have had—bases on the averted side of our moon."

One thing is certain. The above evidence, which could be considerably expanded, indicates that for a solar system which many believe is inaccessible from any other part of the universe, an extraordinary number of unidentified objects have been observed within its boundaries by the most qualified of scientists, none of which can be explained in normal accepted terms, any one of which could have been part of a leapfrogging operation.

Conceivably related to these solar system observations are several recent occurrences within the orbit of this planet. On February 11, 1960, the U.S. Defense Department announced that a mysterious object circling in a "near polar" orbit had been discovered by its radar tracking stations. After two weeks the identity and origin of the so-called "dark satellite" (estimated weight fifteen to eighteen tons) had not been determined. Defense Department spokesmen then advised reporters that the object, which was not emitting radio signals, was believed to be the final stage of a multi-stage USSR rocket launched into orbit around the moon and earth during October, 1959.

Later that same day Professor Alla Masevich, astronomer in charge of seventy Soviet tracking stations, said she "very much doubted" the object was of Russian origin. All USSR earth satellites had been fired into orbits of sixty-five degrees to the equator, nowhere near either pole. "If it was anything as useful as a satellite," advised Professor Masevich, "I would have expected to know about it. But this is the first I have heard of it."

In the midst of considerable news media interest, the next day U.S. Secretary of the Air Force Sharp issued a statement that the object was "probably the casing of an early American Discoverer." Since such a casing would weigh nowhere near fifteen to eighteen tons and a fortnight of careful checking had preceded the earlier statement that it was believed to be Russian, it is understandable why *Newsweek* (July 4, 1960) under the title "The Strange Intruder" should state in part:

> A growing number of scientists are now convinced that Spacetrack (the National Space Control Center, New Bedford, Massachusetts), for all its diligence, may have overlooked at least one space vehicle neither Russian or American, but out of this world—indeed, out of this solar system.
> This satellite, they suspect, is a visitor sent by the "superior beings" of a community of other stars within our Milky Way galaxy.

No statement from any official source, Russian or American, during the past sixteen years has lessened that suspicion.

This "mystery spook satellite" as *Time* (February 22, 1960) described it was not the first strange foreign body orbiting this planet to make headlines. In 1953 new long-range Air Force radar had picked up a huge object six hundred miles out circling the earth near the equator at a speed approaching eighteen thousand miles per hour. Not long after a second one was discovered in orbit about four hundred miles away.

During the summer of 1960, four or five months after the appearance of the strange intruder in a near polar orbit, Grumman Aircraft released a photograph taken above New York of a foreign body, with related positions and movements of neighboring stars

indicated. It was following a course *opposite to earth-launched satellites.*
The *Daily Telegraph* (London, September 3, 1960) reported:

> A mysterious space object which has appeared in the sky over
> New York five times since August 23 has been photographed
> by a tracking camera at the Grumman Aircraft Plant,
> Bethpage, Long Island. Its speed is thought to be about three
> times that of the Satellite Echo I. A spokesman for Grumman
> said the object was photographed at 8:50 P.M. last Thursday as
> it passed over the company's plant in a westerly direction. The
> announcement followed reports that scientists had detected an
> object of similar description over Chicago and various East
> Coast areas late last week. Observers said the object seemed to
> glow with an intermittent reddish light. It travels from east to
> west rather than in the west-to-east path followed by man-
> made satellites.

The *Chicago Daily News* had reported on August 27 that the same
object was seen by Richard Johnson, Director of the Adler Plan-
etarium, at 9:00 P.M. on August 26.

Another series of phenomena conceivably fits into the pattern of
those described above, involving large numbers of people and not
necessarily astronomers and related scientists.

Let us assume for the moment that some unidentified body, natural
or otherwise, passed during the daytime between the sun and the
earth. Just as the moon's passage between those two bodies is known to
cause a solar eclipse, so such an unknown object would cause a "mini"
eclipse, its extent dependent upon two factors: 1) the size of the object,
and 2) its distance from the earth. It so happens that quite a large
number of such unnatural "eclipses" have been recorded during the
past several hundred years, and though many explanations for them
have been offered, they remain essentially inexplicable.

The most dramatic of these took place on a "light but cloudy" day,
March 20, 1886, at 3:00 P.M. in Oshkosh, Wisconsin. Within five
minutes a blackness equal to "midnight" enveloped the city. The
darkness lasted for "eight to ten minutes" during which there were
scenes of panic, runaway horses, people rushing through the streets
and to their homes. Then the day suddenly became as bright as it had
been before.

Most fascinating of all, the "wave of total darkness" moved from
west to east, and subsequently reports came in from towns west of

Oshkosh that the same phenomenon had taken place in that area before
3:00 P.M.

Much the same thing took place in Memphis, Tennessee, at 10:00
A.M. December 2, 1904. In this instance the "intense darkness" lasted
for about fifteen minutes. The *Monthly Weather Review* (32:522)
reported: "We are told that in some quarters a panic prevailed, and
that some were shouting and praying and imagining that the end of the
world had come."

In England two such incidents deserve mention. In broad daylight
on August 19, 1763, a darkness engulfed London that was "greater
than at the great eclipse of 1748." One hundred nineteen years later,
Major J. Herschel, a descendant of the astronomer, reported in *Nature*
(25:289) that a similar occurrence took place at 10:30 A.M. January 22,
1882, in London. (For an extensive list of similar occurrences see
Friedrich H. A. Humboldt's *Cosmos* (1:120), 1845–62.)

One last phenomenon may conceivably tie in with those reported in
this chapter. During the 1920s radio pioneers exploring the
ionosphere—the layer fifty to two hundred miles above the earth that
reflects radio waves around the planet—discovered that although radio
signals penetrating the layer are usually dispersed in space, certain
ones, after delays, were being reflected back.

While radio waves ordinarily circle the earth in less than a second,
in 1928 Størmer, the Norwegian mathematician and geophysicist, and
Van der Pol, the Dutch radio communications authority, recorded
echoes taking three to fifteen seconds. Such delays might indicate that
the signals were being reflected off an unknown object in the vicinity
of the moon. In 1960 the Stanford University astronomer R. N.
Bracewell first proposed that the sequences of these delayed signals
might be caused by a spacecraft from outside our system which was
attempting to establish contact by returning certain of our own signals
to us. Today other scientists are investigating Bracewell's theory in
depth.

17

*During an evening reception of several hundred astronomers
at Victoria, British Columbia, in the summer of 1968,
word spread that just outside the hall
strangely maneuvering lights—UFOs—had been spotted.
The news was met with casual banter
and the giggling sound that often accompanies an embarrassing situation.
Not one astronomer ventured outside
in the summer night to see for himself.*

—Dr. J. Allen Hynek, *Chairman, Dept. of Astronomy, Northwestern
University*

Since shortly after World War II an astounding, in many respects
ludicrous, state of affairs has existed in the field of astronomy and
related disciplines. Although it is scientifically acceptable to spend
billions of dollars annually to investigate the possibility that intelligent
beings may exist outside our solar system, it is considered highly
suspect to explore the possibility that any such intelligent beings may
have succeeded in reaching the immediate vicinity of this planet, or
perhaps even landed on it.

While quite a number of highly qualified scientists have had the
temerity to state that they believe flying saucers are very much a
reality, the only money available for a proper investigation of the
phenomenon is apparently the $20,000 yearly budget allotted in 1975
to Dr. Hynek and his anonymous colleagues at the Center for UFO
Studies, Northwestern University.

In his book *The UFO Experience: A Scientific Inquiry* (1972) Dr.
Hynek, who served for twenty years as Astronomy Consultant to the

U.S. Air Force, quotes a statement by quantum mechanics authority Erwin Schrödinger: "The first requirement of a scientist is that he be curious." Few would disagree with this, yet in actual practice the vitriol and ridicule doled out in support of the Levoissier-type dictum, "No one has ever seen a flying saucer because flying saucers don't exist," has been so violent that discretion in the vast majority of cases proves to be the better part of valor.

It is now nearly thirty years since, during an evening spent with mutual friends, General Jimmy Doolittle, who was in command of the first atomic bomb mission over Japan, remarked that of the UFO incidents occurring during the previous several years approximately ten percent could not be explained in natural terms. They have never been satisfactorily rationalized.

During the intervening years the file has of course built up to gigantic proportions. At the first Astronomical Week held at Barcelona in May, 1965, Professor Hermann Julius Oberth,* who is probably more responsible than any other scientist for getting *Homo sapiens* into orbit, was asked by a reporter, "What have you to tell us about flying saucers? Are they real?" Before a large audience Oberth replied: "We must consider real a fact of which we possess eight thousand certain cases."

On a broad scale it is provocative that in a three-way coincidence, just as mankind appears to be running out of terrestrial time and simultaneously the capability of pursuing an extraterrestrial solution evolves, thousands of persons across the face of the globe claim to have seen artifacts not made by people dwelling on earth.

Let us add up the evidence at either end of the spectrum examined in this text. It has been said by one prominent evolutionist that all of the known fossils bearing on man's origin and ancestry could be put into a normal-sized coffin. Going a step further than the eleven scientists discussed in the early chapters, Sir Wilfrid Le Gros Clark in *Fossil Evidence for Human Evolution* (1964) reiterated even more emphatically that the possibility we will add appreciably to this evidence is very slim indeed:

---

* Author of the two trail-blazing works *The Way to Space Travel* (1929) and *The Rocket into Interplanetary Space* (1934), Dr. Oberth played the key role in the development of the V-1 and V-2 weapons. He believes UFOs are "spaceships from unknown worlds," most probably from a planet of Tau Ceti or Epsilon Eridani. "Obviously the beings who man and fly them are far ahead of us culturally, and if we go about things properly we can learn a lot from them." He estimates that if they would share their knowledge with us, we could reach a scientific level that would normally take 100,000 years to attain.

The chances of finding the fossil remains of actual ancestors, or even representatives of the local geographical group which provided the actual ancestors, are so fantastically remote as not to be worth consideration.

At the other end of the pole, it strains one's credulity far more to dismiss out of hand as fantasy all eight thousand cases of UFO sightings than to believe that in some instances we may be dealing with artifacts from outer space.

And just as one irrefutable piece of fossil evidence—an *unforged* "Piltdown man"—would shore up immeasurably the theory that *Homo sapiens* evolved on earth, so a single incontestable case involving penetration from outside would greatly strengthen the hypothesis that we might have evolved as a species elsewhere in the universe. Weighing all the factors, it is a situation in which one should at least maintain an objective viewpoint.

During the past three years about two thousand UFO case histories were examined by this author. So much has been written about the more impressive of these that there is no point in going over the same ground. Certain incidents emerge vividly from the others, and collectively the ten percent cited by General Doolittle would appear to stand up today as it did around 1950, a figure supported by a statement issued a few years ago by a subcommittee of the American Institute of Astronautics and Aeronautics:

> We find it difficult to ignore the small residue of well-documented but unexplainable cases which form the hardcore of the UFO controversy.

What is worth examining as an entity are the measured statements of a large number of extremely well-positioned individuals who are far more aware of the truth about UFOs than the general public. None is more impressive than that made by Monsieur Robert Galley, French Minister of Defense (Ministre des Armeés) during one of the radio programs broadcast in early 1974 by *France-Inter,* the series which ended abruptly when the remaining tapes were stolen from the network's Paris offices. The following is a transcribed part of the interview:

> *Interviewer:* Mr. Minister, you have mentioned the gendarmie. Now, our listeners have heard, several times in this series, the conclusions reached in the investigations conducted by your

gendarmes—spectacular conclusions: when a witness declares that he has seen a saucer land and that he has seen small humanoids near the saucer, very frequently the gendarmes reach the conclusion that the witness is speaking the truth. What do you yourself think of this?

Minister: Well, of course I should no doubt be a great deal more cautious. But all the same I must say that if your listeners could see for themselves the mass of reports coming in from the airborne gendarmie, the mobile gendarmie, and from the gendarmie charged with the job of conducting investigations, all of which reports are being forwarded by us to the C.N.E.S. (National Center for Space Studies), then they would see that it is all pretty disturbing.

My view about the gendarmie is they are serious people. When they draw up a report, they don't do it haphazardly. If there were only two or three such reports, one might indeed think that perhaps the gendarmie's good faith had been deceived. But I must tell you that in fact the number of these gendarmerie reports is very great, and they are very varied. The whole thing is of course still very fragmentary but I must emphasize that, in this UFO business, it is essential to preserve an extremely open mind."

The minister's remarks are underscored by a statement emanating some time earlier from his fellow countryman General L. M. Chassin, Air Defense Coordinator, Allied Air Forces, Central Europe (NATO):

It is the business of governments to take a hand, if only to avoid the danger of global tragedy such as was revealed by the Soviet complaint to the Security Council recently. For if we persist in refusing to recognize the existence of these unidentified objects, we will end up one fine day, by mistaking them as the guided missiles of an enemy; and the worst will be upon us.

In the light of these remarks it is easier to understand why the late U Thant, while Secretary General of the U.N., publicly voiced the opinion that, except for disarmament, UFOs constituted the most serious question facing the nations of the world; or why Lord Dowding, former Air Chief Marshal of Britain, in the early 1950s stated unequivocally: "I believe absolutely in the existence of flying saucers."

General Paul Stehlin of the French Air Force, A. B. Melville, Commandant-General of the South African Union, Sir George Jones, Air Marshal of Australia, and most recently, in late 1976, General Carlos Cavero, commanding officer of the Spanish Air Force in the Canary Islands, are among unimpeachable witnesses in widely separated parts of the world who have observed UFOs firsthand, each firmly convinced that what he saw could not be explained in natural terms.

A statement that appeared in the *Soviet Weekly* (February 10, 1968) was as disconcerting to the conventional-minded as the comments of French Defense Minister Galley. Further clarifying U Thant's opinion, Professor Felix Zigel of the Moscow Institute of Aviation declared: "Unidentified flying objects are now so firmly established as a problem that an international effort is needed to solve it." He cited a number of observations by USSR government scientists.

Although public "belief" in flying saucers fluctuates up and down depending on the number of incidents in various areas, all of these statements stand unrefuted on the record. If not one more UFO is ever sighted, they will still remain scientifically unexplained.

Two early government communiqués from South America emphasize the global dimensions of the problem. The Brazilian Army Technical School in Rio de Janeiro published an official air force document on December 2, 1954, which concluded:

1. Evidence shows that the saucers are real. No government can afford to ignore the reports and all investigations should be made to determine the identity of any UFO sighted over the country. The problem could be of military interest.
2. The saucers appear to be some kind of revolutionary aircraft. They are not conventional phenomena or illusions. There are too many responsible people involved to say that the whole thing is an hallucination.
3. We do not know where they come from, and we do not know the purpose of their survey. We hope some day to solve the riddle and know the answers.

Eleven years later, on July 7, 1965, the Secretariat of the Argentine Navy released an official communiqué in connection with certain observations made by Argentine, Chilean, and British personnel stationed at bases in Antarctica, conceivably related to the orbiting bodies discussed in the previous chapter.

In a particularly lucid interview reported widely in the world press

Commandant D. M. J. Barrera of the Chilean Air Force Antarctic Base stated:

> It is very rash to give an opinion in the matter, but what we observed was no hallucination or collective psychosis. We are at this base for scientific tasks and what we see we try to analyze from this point of view. But I can say that it was not a star, for it had a very rapid and continuous movement. As far as I am concerned it is a celestial object that I am unable to identify. That it could be an aircraft constructed on this earth I do not believe possible. I belong to the Air Force, and to my knowledge the machines built by man fall far below this, in respect to shape, speed, maneuverability in the air, etc.

Telescopic sightings made the previous November by the Director of the Adhara Observatory in Argentina of an unidentified object which tracked U.S. satellite Echo II across the early evening sky come to mind. All such incidents occurring in the far southern regions help explain remarks made by U.S. Rear Admiral George Dufek on his retiring in the late 1960s as Commander of the Antarctic Research and Exploration Program:

> I think it is very stupid for human beings to think no one else in the universe is as intelligent as we are. Perhaps on other planets there are beings much more advanced. Perhaps that is the importance of the Antarctic. The South Pole is a very valuable scientific laboratory.

In the United States the most paradoxical UFO situation of all exists. More qualified scientists and government personnel have lent credence to the reality of the phenomena than anywhere else, yet at the same time the most persistent, highly emotional campaign has been waged to convince the public that they belong to the lunatic fringe.

A survey conducted in 1971 by *Industrial Research,* a responsible U.S. engineering trade journal, among its professional subscribers revealed that thirty-two percent were convinced that UFOs "must be coming from outer space."

One top authority in this practical field, Dr. James S. Harder, Professor of Engineering at the University of California, concluded after an exhaustive study that they were certainly a "reality" and stressed the "extreme urgency of our learning the technical principles of these crafts."

An aerospace scientist second to none in his field had the opportunity of examining a UFO at close range. Inventor William Lear, while flying in his executive jet, studied the maneuvers for several minutes. He concluded that it was "thousands of years more advanced" than any craft yet developed on this planet. He stated further: "The beings who operate the UFOs must have learned how to neutralize and control gravity," an opinion shared by fellow aircraft manufacturers Grover Loening, Lawrence Bell, and Igor Sikorsky.

Other leading scientists who have expressed strong affirmative views on the subject include Dr. Clyde Tombaugh, discoverer of the planet Pluto, another firsthand UFO observer; Dr. John C. Lilly of dolphin-communication fame; Dr. Seymour Hess, head of the Department of Meteorology at Florida State University; and Nathan Wagner, Missile Chief at White Sands, New Mexico. Both Hess and Wagner were involved in UFO incidents, as was Dr. Henry Carlock, head of the Department of Physics at the University of Mississippi, a colonel in the Air Force Reserve, who sighted what he believed was an extrater-restrial artifact through a 100-power telescope over Jackson, Mississippi.

While it is difficult to resist the "crackpot" denigrating propaganda that floods the news media, it is impossible to brush aside the weight of such scientific evidence on the other side of the fence, especially since it is supported by equally reliable firsthand witnesses.

A partial list of these observers, all of whom were convinced they had seen artifacts that could not be explained in accepted terms—and who in most cases were stunned by what they saw—includes a U.S. Secretary of the Navy, Dan Kimball, and U.S. Admiral Arthur Radford (a joint sighting); the late Richard B. Russell, for many years Chairman of the U.S. Senate Armed Services Committee; Henry Ford II; astronaut James McDivitt during the Gemini IV flight; and Haydon Burns, former Governor of Florida.

In *Migration to the Stars* Dr. Gilfillan states that he finds the evidence of trained airline personnel particularly convincing; here the data is so voluminous that only a few specifics can be mentioned. Director General of the International Air Transport Association Kurt Hammerskjold stated before an assembly of aviation/space reporters in 1966 that, based on firsthand reports he had examined, he was convinced that UFOs were "observation machines from outer space."

Following are five typical incidents involving commercial or military pilots, again on a global basis. An astonishing sighting which hit the pages of *Life* magazine involved nine passengers and two airline officers aboard a Lodestar that left Nairobi West Airport, Kenya, at 7:00 A.M., February 19, 1951. Calculating that the two-hundred-foot-long, bullet-shaped, metal craft moved at a speed of more than a thousand miles an hour, leaving no vapor trail, Captain Bicknell later stated that it was "some kind of flying machine" but that it was "five hundred years ahead of anything we have today." Radio officer D. W. Merrifield expressed the same opinions.

When Major Robert Walker broke the world's altitude record on July 17, 1962, in an X-15 rocket, reaching a height of fifty-eight miles above the U.S., he reported seeing a UFO at the peak of his climb. *Time* magazine (July 27) reported that the astronaut shouted: "There *are* things out there. There absolutely *is!*"

After what was apparently the only recorded case in which a helicopter nearly collided with a UFO, Army Captain Lawrence J. Coyne, a veteran of nineteen years of military flying, told the *Cleveland Enquirer* (October 22, 1973) that he had "never seen anything like it before." The communication system of the helicopter blacked out for ten minutes after the near tragedy. Copilot Arrigo D. Jezzi and crew members confirmed that although they were certain the object was an artifact, its appearance and movements were totally unlike any man-made craft in existence. "It was strange," declared Jezzi. "We're all grown men. We've never seen anything like it."

On a night navigation flight from Ota Airport, Portugal (September 4, 1957), the pilots of four jet fighter bombers were thrown into near panic by a huge unidentified object. Explained Captain J. L. Ferreira (who had fifteen hundred flying hours in jets): "As we were near Coruche the big thing suddenly and very rapidly made what looked like a dive, followed up by a climb in our direction. Then everybody went wild and almost broke formation in the process of crossing over and ahead of the UFO. We were all very excited and I had a hard time to calm things down." Emphasizing the unusual nature of the sighting, Captain Ferreira stated: "Since the first moment we detected the UFO to the final show, a registered time of forty minutes had elapsed, and during it we had ample opportunity to verify every possible explanation for the phenomenon. We've got no conclusions except that after this do not give us the old routine of Venus, balloons, aircraft, and the like which has been given as a general panacea for almost every case of UFOs." During the time the jet fighter pilots were undergoing their harrowing experience, the Coimbra Meteorological Observatory, less than twenty miles from Coruche, registered extraordinary variations in the magnetic field. Recorded diagrams at the observatory bear this out.

The last of the five incidents, which probably received wider publicity than any that has taken place in America, warrants a bit more space because it points up dramatically the reasons why even the most reliable individuals hesitate to report a UFO sighting. It centered around American Airlines pilot Peter Killian, who during twenty years had flown over four million miles.

On a nonstop night flight from Newark Airport to Detroit (February 24, 1959), Captain Killian, copilot John Dee, and stewardesses Edna Lagate and Beverly Pingree, with the thirty-five passengers aboard, observed for over half an hour three lighted unidentified objects flying in precision formation below them. The same objects were observed by the captains of two other American Airliners in the vicinity, by the personnel of three United Airlines planes, and by several ground witnesses in the vicinity of Akron, Ohio.

On landing in Detroit, Captain Killian and several others aboard his plane gave reporters detailed descriptions of what they had seen, thus creating national interest. After three days of silence the Air Technical Intelligence Center released a statement that what had been seen were the stars known as the "Belt of Orion," which could hardly have been situated between the plane and the ground.

When it became obvious that this explanation was totally unacceptable, the USAF released a second statement stating that the three objects were "B-47 bombers being refueled in the air by a KC-97 tanker." Standing firm in the midst of what had become a flaming public row, Captain Killian replied: "If the Air Force wants to believe that, it can. But I know what a B-47 looks like and I know what a KC-97 tanker looks like in operation at night. . . . Those objects were triple the size of a bomber or tanker." (Cross checks on positions and times with the pilots of the other airliners had established a size of approximately 300 feet as compared to a DC-6 size of 117 feet.)

Bringing out an especially odious element in the controversy, Killian continued: "The Air Force has intimated that I had been drinking. I have never had a drink before or during a flight." Whether the seventy-odd additional witnesses were also accused of drinking was not revealed.

When it became apparent that the veteran pilot had no intention of remaining silent, strong pressures were applied. American Airlines, which had arranged some of the early press interviews, advised him he would either have to stop talking or lose his job. Captain Killian had nothing more to say.

Far more important than the UFOs in this and scores of other comparable, if less publicized, happenings is this question: Why, instead of trying to clarify such situations, is every effort made to keep the facts hidden from the public? It is easily understood why millions of people today firmly believe that there is far more to the UFO mystery than has been officially revealed. When one reads through the files, what stands out in case after case is not the unreliability of witnesses but the cavalier and totally unscientific explanations fed the public.

Undoubtedly an unfinished chapter in man's history—over one hundred baffling episodes occurred in Spain alone during 1976—UFOs may in the end prove to be as important as any other body of evidence in repositioning our role in the universe.

Although all of the evidence is not yet in, our search for the origin point of *Homo sapiens* has thus far led us to twenty-five conclusions:

1. In the mid-nineteenth century Charles Robert Darwin encouraged his contemporaries to reexamine their past objectively and dispassionately, helping to free man from nearly two millennia of religious superstition and intellectual sophistry.

2. From the publication of *The Origin of Species* in 1859 until the 1950s the orthodox theory of evolution championed by Thomas Huxley and Ernst Haeckel emphasized direct continuity between *Homo sapiens* and the anthropoid apes, with the search for fossil evidence concentrated on an authentic "missing link" between ourselves and other higher primates.

3. During this same period a number of well-placed scientists claimed that "a being, whose body is replete with features of a basal mammalian simplicity" could not have "sprung from any of those animals in which so much of this simplicity has been lost."

4. During the past quarter century this unorthodox viewpoint has been incorporated into the orthodox theory to a degree where the current scientific consensus favors a separation of man's ancestral line from the primate stem that dates back at least 25 to 30 million years.

5. A high percentage of evolutionists today believe that Proconsul, whose fossil remains are of that period, was of sufficient basal mammalian simplicity to have been a common ancestor to both *Homo sapiens* and the anthropoid apes, the two species following their own separate evolutionary developments.

6. About an equal number of specialists currently view Proconsul as too "apelike" to have been an ancestor of man. These scientists believe that either some earlier undiscovered primate was a common ancestor to *Homo sapiens* and the anthropoids, or that a separate cleavage of

Homo sapiens from the primate stem took place 60 to 70 million years ago.

7. All such opinions as to what occurred prior to 25 to 30 million years ago are necessarily hypothetical, as there is no fossil evidence that proves any of them. Although few scientists would claim that *Homo sapiens* reached full evolutionary development prior to that date, there is strong support for the view he may have assumed an upright position by then.

8. Points 4 through 7 constitute the first half of the most inexplicable paradox in our past, for while man may have pursued a separate evolutionary track for 25 to 30 million years or longer, the supporting fossil evidence is virtually nonexistent (the second half of the paradox). For example:

9. There is no proven, accepted fossil evidence of man's ancestral existence on this planet during the Tertiary Period (25 to 30 million years ago to 500,000 years ago), as pointed out earlier in this book by Weidersheim, Fothergill, and Zuckerman. Despite the belief that such Tertiary remains will eventually be found in Africa, none to date have been discovered.

10. *Australopithecus.* The unearthing of these fossils aroused great initial interest because they were found in deposits dating from nearly 2 million to c. 800,000 years ago, with some dates not fully established. Although popular writers still maintain that Australopithecus was directly ancestral to man, it has been impossible to find any qualified specialist who during the past decade has supported this position. The scientific consensus appears to have swung to the opinion expressed by Dr. Louis B. Leakey in 1966: "They were not ancestors of man, but an evolutionary sideline."

11. *Pithecanthropus.* With no fossil evidence of any immediate precursors of Pithecanthropus, 500,000 to 400,000 years ago, and with the next 200,000 to 300,000 years represented by only two broken skulls—both found in Europe—it again appears that the scientific consensus is moving in the "sideline-that-became-extinct" direction.

12. *Neanderthal man* (c. 70,000 years ago). Although J. Bronowski in *The Ascent of Man* expresses the opinion that Neanderthal man was a direct ancestor of *Homo sapiens,* it has been impossible to find any qualified evolutionist who during the past ten to fifteen years has supported this position.

13. *Cro-Magnon man* (c. 30,000 years ago). It has yet to be firmly established that he was a true *Homo sapiens.*

14. Examining points 4 through 13, there would appear to be no

proven, accepted fossil evidence of man's direct ancestry up to the beginning of the Holocene epoch (c. 10,000 years ago) or, if one includes Cro-Magnon man as *Homo sapiens,* up to 30,000 years ago.

15. While some authorities anticipate additional clarifying fossil evidence, others support the view expressed by Le Gros Clark: "The chances of finding the fossil remains of *actual* ancestors, or even representatives of the local geographical group which provided the actual ancestors, are so fantastically remote as not to be worth consideration."

16. The above points deal with structural comparative anatomy. Turning to the psychozoatic aspects of man, one finds Sir Julian Huxley and others proposing a far wider gap between *Homo sapiens* and all other primates than had previously been suggested by evolutionists: "Man is indeed a new and unique *kind* of organism and has stepped over the threshold of a quite new phase or sector of the evolutionary process."

17. Throughout the world a large portion of mankind's religious and legendary heritage—what might be termed the metaphysical aspects of our past—is more readily explicable as an extraterrestrial evolution rather than one that took place on earth.

18. At an increasing pace the evidence pertaining to the capabilities and accomplishments of *Homo sapiens* during the Holocene epoch bears less and less relationship to the orthodox concept of early man as a primitive barbarian, one step removed from the caves and bogs, two steps removed from the apes. A growing number of facts and artifacts, essentially diffusionist in nature, cannot be fitted into this concept.

19. With the current scientific consensus supporting the opinion that *Homo sapiens* attained his present mental development at least one million years ago, it is difficult to explain why man waited until c. 8,000 B.C. before taking off culturally at such a breathtaking pace.

20. Also inexplicable is why the human population explosion that occurred during the same period did not begin earlier.

21. On the basis of evidence accumulated during the past century, and especially since World War II, a majority of astronomers and scientists working in related disciplines believe today that the odds are in favor of intelligent beings existing outside our solar system, a high percentage of whom are probably far more advanced scientifically than ourselves. A number of these authorities have expressed the opinion that, given universal evolutionary and physical laws, at least some of these intelligent beings may be very much like *Homo sapiens.*

22. During the past three centuries a number of mysterious objects have been telescopically sighted within our solar system, in many instances by world-famous astronomers, none of which has been satisfactorily explained.

23. While unidentified flying objects have occasionally been reported in the vicinity of the earth since ancient times, during the past thirty years these reports have increased on a worldwide scale to astonishing proportions. Contrary to popular opinion, a large percentage of these sightings have involved extremely reliable witnesses and/ or those with special technical skills.

24. Within the past two decades man has not only proved himself capable of leaving this planet, but has developed the technical skills and resources necessary for a large-scale colonization of our solar system. With the addition of thermonuclear energy this conceivably could be extended to the entire Milky Way.

25. In what could be a three-way coincidence or possibly related facets of a broader universal evolutionary process than the terrestrial one propounded by Darwin and his followers, during the same recent period when man has proved himself a potential interplanetary creature and evidence of conceivable "outside" interest in earthly affairs has stepped up at a remarkable rate, more and more scientists have become convinced that a combination of insoluble problems will render this planet virtually uninhabitable within the next two hundred years or less.

Although one may disagree with the conclusion that *Homo sapiens* may have evolved as a fully developed species somewhere else and then come to this planet in relatively recent times as part of a universal colonizing and evolutionary process, it is difficult to quarrel with the evidence. It is based on research done in the main by scientists of the highest order.

In my own research, which with the exception of the maps has been reportorial, the biggest surprise is the twenty-five-year time lag between scientific consensus and current popular views regarding *Homo sapiens'* evolution. A quarter century seems inordinate and one suspects that, wittingly or otherwise, when in a cross-sectional sampling of about fifty men under forty three-quarters of them believe that *Homo sapiens* descended from apes, the facts have been kept from the public.

However, looking toward the future, one cannot do better than follow the advice of Francis Bacon:

> For as God was the help of our reason to illuminate us, so should we likewise turn it every way, that we may be more capable of understanding His mysteries; provided only that the mind be enlargened, according to its capacity, to the grandeur of the mysteries, and not the mysteries contracted to the narrowness of the mind.

Akurgal, Ekrem. *Ancient Civilizations and Ruins of Turkey.* Istanbul: Mobil Oil Türk A.S., 1969.

Antoniadi, Eugene Michel. *L'Astronomie égyptienne depuis les temps les plus reculés, jusqu'à la fin de l'époque alexandrine.* Paris: Gauthier-Villars, 1934.

Ardrey, Robert. *African Genesis.* New York: Atheneum, 1961.

Aurousseau, M. *The Rendering of Geographical Names.* 1957. Reprint. Westport, Conn.: Greenwood, 1975.

Bacon, E., ed. *Vanished Civilizations of the Ancient World.* New York: McGraw-Hill, 1963. See Lhote and Sieveking.

Bailey, James. *The God-Kings and the Titans.* New York: St. Martin's, 1973.

Bartholomew's Gazetteer of the British Isles. 9th ed. Edinburgh: John Bartholomew & Son Ltd., 1966.

Bass, George Fletcher. *Archaeology Under Water.* Baltimore: Penguin, 1972.

———, and Winslow, Richard K. *A History of Seafaring Based on Underwater Archaeology.* New York: Walker, 1972.

Beer, G. R. de. *Embryos and Ancestors.* New York: Oxford U. Press, 1958.

Bergsoe, P. *The Gilding Process and the Metallurgy of Copper and Gold among the Pre-Columbian Indians.* Copenhagen: Ingeniørvidenskabelige Skrister, 1938.

———. *The Metallurgy and Technology of Gold and Platinum among the Pre-Columbian Indians.* Copenhagen: Ingeniørvidenskabelige Skrister, 1937.

Berndt, Ronald M., and Berndt, Catherine H. *The World of the First Australians.* London: Angus & Robertson, 1964.

Berriman, A. E. *Historical Metrology.* Westport, Conn.: Greenwood, 1953.

Bisschop, Eric de. *Tahiti Nui.* New York: McDowell-Obolensky, 1959.

Borlase, William. *The Dolmens of Ireland.* 3 vols. London: Chapman and Hall, 1897.

Borst, Lyle B. *Science.* November, 1969.

Boule, Pierre Marcellin, with Vallois, H. V. *Fossil Men.* London: Thames and Hudson, 1967.

Bovill, E. W. *The Golden Trade of the Moors.* New York: Oxford U. Press, 1970.

Brewer, E. Cobham. *Brewer's Dictionary of Phrase and Fable.* New York: Harper & Row, 1971.

Bronowski, J. *The Ascent of Man.* Boston: Little, Brown, 1973.

Brooks, W. R. *Science.* 31 July 1896.

Brown, J. Macmillan. *The Riddle of the Pacific.* London: T. Fisher, Unwin, 1924.

Browne, Thomas. *Religio Medici.* Edited by J. Winny. New York: Cambridge U. Press, 1963.

Burn, A. R. *Minoans, Philistines, and Greeks.* New York: Knopf, 1930.

Bushnell, G. H. S. *The First Americans: The Pre-Columbian Civilizations.* New York: McGraw-Hill, 1968.

Chapman, Robert. *UFO: Flying Saucers over Britain?* St. Albans: Mayflower Books, 1969.

Clark, Wilfrid E. Le Gros. *Early Forerunners of Man.* London: Baillière, Tindall and Cox, 1934.

——. *Fossil Evidence for Human Evolution: An Introduction to the Study of Paleoanthropology.* Chicago: U. of Chicago Press, 1964.

Clement, Geneviève. "The Rediscovery of Spirulina." *Ceres* (UN), August 1971, 44–46.

Concise Oxford Dictionary of English Place-Names, The. New York: Oxford U. Press, 1960.

Cope, E. D. *The Origin of the Fittest: Essays on Evolution and the Primary Factors of Organic Evolution.* New York: Cerno, 1974.

Cottrell, Leonard, ed. *Concise Encyclopedia of Archaeology, The.* New York: Hawthorn, 1974.

Darlington, C. D. *The Evolution of Man and Society.* New York: Simon and Schuster, 1970.

Darwin, Charles. *The Descent of Man and Selection in Relation to Sex.* Detroit: Gale, 1974.

——. *The Origin of Species.* New York: Macmillan, 1962.

Darwin, Erasmus. *Temple of Nature.* New York: British Book Center, 1973.

——. *Zoonomia: or the Laws of Organic Life.* New York: AMS Press, n.d.

Darwin, F. *The Life and Letters of Charles Darwin.* 2 vols. New York: R. West, 1973.

Davies, A. M. *Evolution and Its Modern Critics.* London: Thomas Murby and Co., 1937.

De La Vega, Garcilaso. *Royal Commentaries of the Incas and General History of Peru.* Austin: U. of Texas Press, 1969.

Donnelly, Ignatius. *Atlantis: The Antediluvian World.* New York: Harper & Brothers, 1949.

Encyclopaedia Britannica. 1976 and 1968 eds.

Farb, Peter. *Man's Rise to Civilization as Shown by the Indians of North America from Primeval Times to the Coming of the Industrial State.* New York: Dutton, 1968.

Fell, H. Barraclough. *Harvard Gazette,* November 1974.

——. *America B.C.* New York: Quadrangle/New York Times Book Co., 1977.

——. *The Epigraphic Society.* "Occasional Publications," Arlington, Mass.

Fisher, Ronald. *The Genetical Theory of Natural Selection.* New York: Dover, 1958.

Fletcher, W. W. *Modern Man Looks at Evolution.* London: Fontana Books, 1974.

Flying Saucer Review. London, 1954–1976.

Ford, E. B. "Problems in the Evolution of Geographical Races," in *Evolution as a Process,* edited by Julian Huxley, A. C. Hardy, and E. B. Ford. London: 1954.

Fort, Charles. *Lo!* New York: Ace Books, 1973.

Fothergill, Philip G. *Evolution and Christians.* London: Longmans, 1961.

——. *Historical Aspects of Organic Evolution.* London: Longmans, 1952.

——. *Life and Its Origin.* London: Longmans, 1958.

Gallenkamp, Charles. *Maya: The Riddle and Rediscovery of a Lost Civilization.* New York: McKay, 1976.

Gates, R. R. *Human Ancestry from a Genetical Point of View.* London: Cambridge, Mass.: Harvard U. Press, 1948.

Gilfillan, Edward S., Jr. *Migration to the Stars.* New York and Washington: Robert B. Luce, 1975.

Glob, P. V. *The Bog People.* New York: Ballantine, 1975.

Gordon, Cyrus. *Before Columbus.* New York: Crown, 1971.

Gould, Stephen Jay. "Man and Other Animals." *Natural History.* August/September 1975, 24–26, 28–30.

Grollenberg, L. H. *Atlas of the Bible.* London: Thomas Nelson & Sons, 1956.

Haddon, A. C. *Migrations of Peoples in the South-West Pacific.* Melbourne: 1923.

Haeckel, Ernst. *History of Creation.* 4th ed. London: Kegan Paul, 1892.

Hapwood, A. T. "Miocene Primates from British East Africa." *Annual Magazine of Natural History,* series 10, vol. 11 (1933): 96.

———. "Miocene Primates from Kenya." *Linnaean Society of Zoology,* 1933.

Hawkins, Gerald S. *Beyond Stonehenge.* New York: Harper & Row, 1973.

———, and White, John B. *Stonehenge Decoded.* New York: Doubleday, 1965.

Hencken, Hugh. *The Archaeology of Cornwall.* London: Methuen, 1932.

Heyerdahl, Thor. *Aku-Aku.* New York: Ballantine, 1974.

———. *Kon-Tiki.* New York: Rand McNally, 1951.

———. *Sea Routes to Polynesia.* New York: Rand McNally, 1968.

Hill, W. C. Osman. *Man's Ancestry—A Primer of Human Phylogeny.* London: William Heinemann Medical Books, 1954.

———. *Primates: Comparative Anatomy and Taxonomy.* 8 vols. New York: Halstead Press, 1955–1970.

Honoré, Pierre. *In Quest of the White Gods.* New York: Putnam, 1963.

Howells, William. *The Pacific Islanders.* New York: Scribner's, 1973.

Hübrecht, A. A. W. *The Descent of the Primates.* New York: Scribner's, 1897.

Humboldt, F. H. A. *Cosmos* (1–120). Paris, 1845–1862.

Huxley, Julian. "Destiny of Man" series. Sunday *Times* (London), July/September 1958.

———. *Evolution, The Modern Synthesis.* New York: Hafner, 1975.

Huxley, Thomas H. *Man's Place in Nature.* Ann Arbor: U. of Mich. Press, 1959.

Hynek, J. Allen. *The UFO Experience: A Scientific Inquiry.* Chicago: Henry Regnery, 1972.

Imperial Dictionary of Universal Biography. London: William Mackenzie, n.d.

Irwin, Constance. *Fair Gods and Stone Faces.* New York: St. Martin's, 1963.

Jeans, James H. *The Mysterious Universe.* New York: AMS Press, 1976.

Jones, Frederic Wood. *Structure and Function as Seen in the Foot.* London: Baillière, Tindall and Cox, 1944.

———. *Hallmarks of Mankind.* London: Routledge & Kegan Paul, 1948.

———. *The Hand.* London: J. and A. Churchill, 1920.

———. *Life and Living.* London: Kegan Paul and Co., 1939.

———. *Man's Place Among the Mammals.* London: E. Arnold & Co., 1929.

———. *The Problem of Man's Ancestry.* London: S.P.C.K., 1918.

Keith, Arthur. *The Antiquity of Man.* 2 vols. New York: Gordon Press, n.d.

———. *A New Theory of Human Evolution.* Gloucester, Mass.: Peter Smith, 1968.

Keyhoe, Major Donald E. *Aliens from Space.* Garden City, N.Y.: Doubleday, 1973.

Kurtén, Björn. *The Ice Age.* New York: Putnam, 1972.

Le Bon, Gustave. *The Crowd.* New York: Viking, 1960.

Lhote, Henri. "The Fertile Sahara." In *Vanished Civilizations of the Ancient World,* edited by E. Bacon. New York: McGraw-Hill, 1963.

Lloyd, G. E. R. *Early Greek Science: Thales to Aristotle.* Edited by M. I. Finley. New York: Norton, 1971.

"Looking For Life Out There." *Time,* 13 December 1971, 42–47.

Lyell, Charles. *Principles of Geology.* 3 vols. 1830. New York: Harcourt, Brace, Jovanovich, Johnson Reprint, 1971.

McDonald, D. *The Oceanic Languages: Their Grammatical Structure, Vocabulary and Origin.* London: 1907.

Mallowan, M. E. L. *Early Mesopotamia and Iran.* London: Thames and Hudson, 1965.

Massingham, H. J. *Downland Man.* New York: George H. Doran, n.d.

Michell, John. *City of Revelation.* London: Garnstone Press, 1972.

———. *The Old Stones of Land's End.* London: Garnstone Press, 1974.

———. *The View Over Atlantis.* London: Garnstone Press, 1969.

Mivart, St. George. *Man and Apes. An Exposition of Structural Resemblances and Differences.* London: Robert Hardwicke, 1873.

Montagu, Ashley. *Man, His First Million Years.* New York: New American Library, 1957.

National Aeronautics and Space Administration (NASA). "Chronological Catalogue of Reported Lunar Events." 1968.

Negev, Avraham. *Archaeological Encyclopedia of the Holy Land.* London: Weidenfeld and Nicolson, 1972.

Oberth, Hermann Julius. *The Rocket into Interplanetary Space.* 1934.

———. *The Way to Space Travel.* Paris: 1929.

Osborn, Fairfield. *Our Plundered Planet.* Boston: Little, Brown, 1948.

———. *Limits of the Earth.* Boston: Little, Brown, 1953.

Osborn, Henry Fairfield. "Recent Discoveries Relating to the Origin and Antiquity of Man." *Science* 65 (1927): 481–88.

———. *The Origin and Evolution of Life.* London: G. Bell & Son, 1918.

Oxford Atlas, The. London: Oxford University Press, 1961.

Oxford Classical Dictionary, The. New York: Oxford U. Press, 1949.

Oxford English Dictionary, The. New York: Oxford U. Press, 1933.

Perry, W. J. *The Origin of Oceanic Culture.* Melbourne: 1923.

Petrie, W. M. Flinders. *The Pyramids and Temples of Gizeh.* London: Field & Tuer, 1883.

Piggott, Stuart. *Ancient Europe: From the Beginnings of Agriculture to Classical Antiquity.* Chicago: Aldine, 1966.

———. *British Prehistory.* New York: Oxford U. Press, 1949.

Pilot Books of the World. British Admiralty.

Proctor, Richard Anthony. *The Great Pyramid: Observatory, Tomb, and Temple.* London: Chatto & Windus, 1883.

Rafinesque, C. S. *The American Nations.* Philadelphia, 1836.

Ramsay, R. H. *No Longer on the Map.* New York: Viking, 1972.

Random House Dictionary of the English Language (unabridged). New York: Random House, 1966.

Reed, Alma. *The Ancient Past of Mexico.* New York: Crown, 1966.

Rees, Alwyn and Brinley. *Celtic Heritage: Ancient Ireland and Wales.* Levittown, N.Y.: Transatlantic, 1975.

Renfrew, Colin. *Before Civilization.* New York: Knopf, 1973.

Ronan, Colin. *Lost Discoveries: The Forgotten Science of the Ancient World.* New York: McGraw-Hill, 1973.

Santillana, Giorgio de. *Origins of Scientific Thought: From Anaximander to Plotinus, 600 B.C. to A.D. 300.* Chicago: U. of Chicago Press, 1961.

Shaw, George Bernard. *Back to Methuselah.* 1922. Reprint. New York: Oxford U. Press, 1947.

Sieveking, Gale. "Migration of the Megaliths." In *Vanished Civilizations of the Ancient World,* edited by E. Bacon. New York: McGraw-Hill, 1963.

Smith, Grafton Elliot. *The Migrations of Early Culture.* Manchester: University Press, 1929.

Smith, S. W. *Hawaiki: The Original Home of the Maori.* 3rd ed. Christchurch, N. Z.: Whitcombe & Tombs, 1910.

Smyth, Charles Piazzi. *Life and Work at the Great Pyramid.* Edinburgh: Edmonton & Douglas, 1867.

———. *Our Inheritance in the Great Pyramid.* 5th ed. London: Charles Burnet and Co., 1890.

Stewart, George R. *American Place-Names.* New York: Oxford U. Press, 1970.

———. *Names on the Land.* Boston: Houghton Mifflin, 1958.

Stone, Irving. *Clarence Darrow for the Defense.* New York: Garden City Publishing Company, 1941.

Straus, William L., Jr. "The Riddle of Man's Ancestry." *Quarterly Review of Biology* 24 (Sept., 1949), 200–23.

Tanzer, C., with Eisman, L. *Biology and Human Progress.* Englewood Cliffs, N.J.: Prentice-Hall, 1976.

Taylor, Richard. *New Zealand and Its Inhabitants.* London: William MacIntosh, 1870.

Teilhard de Chardin, Pierre. *The Future of Man.* New York: Harper & Row, 1964.

Temple, Robert K. *The Sirius Mystery: Was Earth Visited by Intelligent Beings from a Planet in the System of the Star Sirius?* New York: St. Martin's, 1975.

Thom, Alexander. *Megalithic Sites in Britain.* New York: Oxford U. Press, 1967.

Times Atlas of the World. London, 1965.

Times Index-Gazetteer of the World. London, 1965.

Tompkins, Peter. *Secrets of the Great Pyramid,* with appendix by Livio Catullo Stecchini. New York: Harper & Row, 1971.

Toynbee, Arnold. *A Study of History.* 1 vol. ed. New York: Oxford U. Press, 1972.

Treager, E. *The Maori in Asia.* Wellington, 1886.

Von Däniken, Erich. *Chariots of the Gods?* New York: Putnam, 1970.

Von Wuthenau, Alexander. *The Art of Terracotta Pottery in Pre-Columbian Central and South America.* New York: Crown, 1969.

Waddington, C. H. *Introduction to Modern Genetics.* London: Allen & Unwin, 1939.

———. *Principles of Embryology.* London: Allen & Unwin, 1956.

Weidersheim, R. *The Structure of Man, An Index to His Past History.* New York: Macmillan, 1895.

Wendt, Herbert. *Before the Deluge.* New York: Doubleday, 1968.

———. *From Ape to Adam: The Search for the Evolution of Man.* Indianapolis: Bobbs-Merrill, 1973.

Wertime, Theodore. "Man's First Encounters with Metallurgy." *Science,* December 1964.

Zigel, Felix. *Soviet Weekly,* 10 February 1968, 3.

Zuckerman, S. *Functional Affinities of Man, Monkeys and Apes.* London: 1933.

———. "Correlation of Changes in Evolution of Higher Primates," *Evolution as a Process,* edited by Julian Huxley, A. C. Hardy, and E. B. Ford. London: 1954.